9.95

KINLOCH HOURN

Glen Garry

Loch Quoich

Gairich

Glen Kingie

gurr na Ciche

Sron a'Choire Ghairbh

Loch Lochy

A82

Glen Dessarry

Glen Pean

Loch Arkaig

CLUNES

Sgurr nan
Coireachan

Gulvain

Glen Mallie

Glen Loy

GLENFINNAN

SPEAN BRIDGE

TO KINGUSSIE. (A86)

B 8005

A82

ar Bheag

A830

A861

Loch Eil

FORT WILLIAM

Cona Glen

Glen Scaddle

Glen Gour

CORRAN

Ferry

To TYNDRUM (A82)

Garbh Bheinn

ert

ch Bheinn

Loch Linnhe

▲ PRINCIPAL SUMMITS   LAND OVER 600m.   LAND OVER 300m.

Kms.   0   5   10   15   20   25   30   35   40

WESTERN HIGHLANDS - SOUTH

Scottish Mountaineering Club
District Guide Books

THE WESTERN HIGHLANDS

General Editor: A. C. D. SMALL

DISTRICT GUIDE BOOKS

Southern Highlands
Central Highlands
Western Highlands
Northern Highlands
Islands of Scotland
Island of Skye
The Cairngorms
Southern Uplands
Mountains of Scotland

Munro's Tables

SCOTTISH MOUNTAINEERING CLUB
DISTRICT GUIDE BOOKS

THE
Western Highlands

by Donald Bennet

THE SCOTTISH MOUNTAINEERING CLUB

EDINBURGH

First published in Britain in 1974 by
THE SCOTTISH MOUNTAINEERING TRUST

First Edition, December 1931
Second Edition 1932
Third Edition revised 1947
Fourth Edition revised 1964
Fifth Edition 1983

ISBN 0 907521 07 X

Filmset by Advanced Filmsetters (Glasgow) Ltd
Printed by Bell and Bain Ltd
Bound by Hunter & Foulis Ltd

CONTENTS

ILLUSTRATIONS

MAPS

drawn by James Renny

ACKNOWLEDGEMENTS

The writing of this guide book would have been very much more difficult had it not been for the willing assistance of several friends.

I am particularly indebted to Scott Johnstone, the author of the previous edition of *The Western Highlands* guide, for much helpful information and his contribution of the section on the geology of the district. All guide book authors owe much to their predecessors, and I have merely followed in the footsteps of Scott Johnstone and James Parker before him, and added a little more to the knowledge and understanding of the Western Highlands which was contained in their books.

My wife Anne, Bob Hillcoat and Professor William Donaldson have been good companions on the rough and remote hills of the west. The Professor has been particularly helpful in placing his total knowledge of the lesser mountains of the area, the Corbetts, at my disposal. John Hinde of Outward Bound Locheil has also provided useful information.

Two contributions to the rock climbing information in this guide book deserve special mention: Norman Tennent on Kintail, and John Mackenzie on Glen Strathfarrar, Strathconon and the northern perimeter.

Finally, I thank Jim Renny for his excellent maps, drawn specially for this book, and Alex Small for the helpful advice that he gave in his capacity as General Editor of this series of District Guide Books.

INTRODUCTION

The area described in this guide book under the title *The Western Highlands* is that part of the Scottish mainland to the west of the Firth of Lorne, Loch Linnhe and the Great Glen from the southern tip of Morvern to the well-defined valley which crosses the north of Scotland from the Cromarty Firth through Strath Bran and Glen Carron to the west coast at Loch Carron.

A glance at a map shows the principal geographical characteristic of this area, a series of parallel glens running from east to west with some long ranges of mountains between them. The watershed between east and west flowing rivers is in most cases quite near the west coast, in places as close as five or six kilometres, so that there are many long straths draining east to the Great Glen, and short steep glens dropping to the western seaboard.

This east-west orientation of the country is emphasised along the west coast where several long and narrow sea-lochs penetrate into the mountainous interior. Some of these sea-lochs such as Loch Nevis, Loch Hourn and Loch Duich are surrounded by steep mountains, and they are among the grandest examples in Scotland of the classic combination of sea, loch and mountain landscape.

The highest mountains of the Western Highlands are in the north, around Glen Affric and Glen Cannich, and remote from the west coast. The steepest and most rugged mountains, however, are near the west coast, in Kintail, Knoydart and the extreme western part of Lochaber. It is characteristic of the area as a whole that its western half is more mountainous than the eastern part in which the glens are long and open, the hills (with a few notable exceptions) smooth and rounded and the hillsides above the Great Glen forested for much of the length of Loch Lochy, Loch Oich and Loch Ness.

On the other hand the western part is characterised by the rough and inhospitable nature of much of the country, which is a confusion of deep narrow glens, remote lochs, tumbling streams, steep crags and rugged mountains. This is the part of the Western Highlands that epitomises the area as a whole. The mountains may not be as high as those of the Cairngorms or central Lochaber; there may be few of the great cliffs and buttresses that give Glencoe its reputation; but for those who seek solitude in wild and remote places, there can be no more enticing part of Scotland.

Only three public roads penetrate through the area from east to west, and although there are numerous small towns and villages around its perimeter, there is very little habitation in the hinterland. Much of the Western Highlands can justifiably be regarded as wilderness in the generally accepted sense of that word: substantial tracts of land which are uninhabited and which show few if any signs of man's activities, past or present. Not all the present wilderness areas of the Western Highlands have always been such. There are many glens which were once populated but now, as a result of the Clearances and other factors, are deserted, and this must be a cause for regret. It is a sobering thought to look at the ruined houses at Carnoch at the head of Loch Nevis and reflect that once several families lived there with enough able-bodied men (so it is said) to field a shinty team. Now the fields, once dug and drained, are overgrown by rank grass and reeds, and the little walled gardens beside the houses are smothered by nettles. It should not be a cause for pride that so many of the glens of the Western Highlands are now regarded as wilderness areas.

Mountaineering

The Western Highlands are predominantly hill-walkers' country, and there is a great variety of mountains and long cross-country paths and tracks for the hill-walker and backpacker. Many old drove roads and rights-of-way thread their ways through the glens and over passes, and in addition there are stalkers' paths leading up many of the hills and corries. The climber is seldom at a loss for some path or track up which to start his day's climbing. Unfortunately many of these paths are now in a state of some disrepair, for although they may well have been originally well built with good foundations and drains, they receive little attention nowadays. At the same time as some of the old-established paths are deteriorating due to lack of maintenance, new roads are being bulldozed up the glens in the interests of forestry, agriculture or stalking. These new roads are in general a scar on the landscape, as for example in Glen Dessarry and Gleann Lichd (Kintail).

Once the paths and tracks are left behind, the climber is likely to find that the terrain of the Western Highland mountains is pretty rough; rocky in some places and boggy in others. It is the author's opinion that one has to make quite an effort to keep up with Naismith's time-honoured formula of three miles per hour on the level, plus two thousand feet per hour going uphill. This formula may be converted to metric units with fair accuracy as five kilometres per hour on the level, plus six hundred metres per hour (or ten metres per minute) going uphill.

There are only a few places in the Western Highlands where there is good rock or ice climbing. This is surprising, for many of the mountains are very rocky and rugged. However, in most cases there are few continuously steep and high crags, and the long walking distances to some of them put them beyond the range that rock-climbers are prepared to walk in search of their sport.

There are, of course, exceptions, none more obvious than Garbh Bheinn in Ardgour. This magnificent mountain has a superb array of ridges, buttresses and gullies on its north-east face, and it is worth many a visit. In Knoydart, Ladhar Bheinn has a fine cirque of cliffs at the head of Coire Dhorrcail, but they are very vegetatious and best suited for winter climbing on the rather rare occasions when a hard frost and good ice conditions prevail. In a neighbouring corrie above Barrisdale there is a good expanse of slabs on An Caisteal.

In Kintail there are climbs, both rock and ice, on The Saddle, the Five Sisters and Beinn Fhada, but none of these have become classics for the rock is a vegetatious schist and none of the winter routes done so far have the length, difficulty or character to put them in the top classification. Further north there are a few climbs on the Glen Strathfarrar and Strathconon mountains, and at the northern edge of the area described in this guide book there are low-level crags near the foot of Strathconon and Strathpeffer which have given good rock climbs.

The usual grading system is used in this book. The explanation of the winter grades is as follows:

Grade I. Straightforward snow climbs with no pitches in adequate snow conditions. They may have cornice difficulties or dangerous outruns in the event of a fall.
Grade II. Gullies containing minor pitches, or high-angled snow, with difficult cornices to finish. Easy buttresses which under winter snow

cover provide continuous difficulty. Equates to a technical standard of Difficult to Very Difficult.

Grade III. Serious climbs which should only be attempted by parties experienced in winter climbing. Equates to a technical standard of Very Difficult to Severe.

Grade IV. Long routes of sustained Severe standard and shorter climbs with short sections of harder standard.

Grade V. Long routes of sustained difficulty giving major expeditions which should only be attempted in favourable conditions.

Transport

Most climbers rely on their own cars to get to and from the mountains, but for those without cars the rather tenuous public transport services of the Western Highlands will have to suffice. These include rail, bus, post-bus and ferry services, and an attempt has been made in this guide book to indicate services which are at present available. Inevitably these services and their timetables will change, and the information in this book will become out of date. The comprehensive guide published by the Highlands and Islands Development Board entitled *Getting Around the Highlands and Islands* contains timetables for all services in the area covered by this book and is published each year, so it remains up to date. This guide is absolutely invaluable to anyone using public transport in the north-west of Scotland. It is available at stores and bookshops in the Highlands, and can also be obtained from The Highlands and Islands Development Board, Bridge House, 27 Bank Street, Inverness IV1 1QR.

Accommodation

With so many climbers using their own cars, the need for accommodation in the immediate vicinity of the mountains is not as great as it once was when hotels such as Cluanie Inn, Tomdoun and the Stage House Inn at Glenfinnan were noted as climbers' hotels. Now, with the convenience of one's own car, it is possible to base oneself at some suitable centre and explore from there. Such centres include Strontian, Invergarry (or Laggan) and the head of Loch Duich, where there are shops, hotels, camp and caravan sites, cottages and caravans to let and bed and breakfast houses. In addition to the many recognised camp and caravan sites, there are almost unlimited opportunities for wild camping, though this should not be taken as an indication that camping will be permitted anywhere. It is always best to seek permission, particularly if one is in the neighbourhood of any farm or cottage. See Appendix III.

Information about bed and breakfast, caravans and cottages to let can be obtained from local tourist offices in the larger towns and villages such as Fort William, Strontian and Kyle of Lochalsh. More detailed information about accommodation, hotels and youth hostels is listed in the following chapters.

Bothies

One of the factors that has somewhat changed the character of West Highland hill-walking in recent years has been the renovation of many deserted and derelict cottages which are now available as simple open shelters. The work of renovation and rebuilding has been carried out by the dedicated voluntary efforts of the Mountain Bothies Association and other climbers and walkers, with the permission of the landowners concerned who allow the cottages to be used as simple unlocked shelters. (In the stalking season the use of these bothies by climbers may be discouraged).

There can be no doubt that the existence of these bothies in the Western Highlands (there are about twenty of them) has made it possible for climbers and cross-country walkers to find reasonable shelter in some very remote corners. To stay for a few nights in one of these cottages enables one to enter fully into the spirit of the lonely Highland glens and mountains, and to experience for a few days the isolation in which, until a few decades ago, many shepherds and keepers lived for much of their lives.

On the other hand, it must be conceded that the appearance of these bothies has to some extent modified the uncompromising wilderness quality of parts of the Western Highlands, enabling climbers and walkers nowadays to find dry shelter in places where ten or twenty years ago they would have had to camp and brave the elements and the midges. It is also certain that the existence of these bothies in their renovated state has been to some extent responsible for the increase in the numbers of climbers and walkers, particularly organised parties, going to the furthest corners of the Western Highlands. It is not uncommon to find a remote little cottage occupied by a large school party, a situation which can completely destroy the sense of peace and solitude which such a place should embody. It may not be out of place, therefore, to suggest that those who use the bothies for shelter should not only respect the facilities which they provide by causing no damage and leaving no litter, but should also have regard for the more intangible qualities of these cottages and their place in the landscape and history of the Highlands.

Rights-of-way

It is appropriate in a guide book dealing with the Western Highlands to say a few words about rights-of-way, for they provide invaluable routes through most of the glens where there are no roads. A public right-of-way is defined as a right of passage, open to the public, over private property by a route which is more or less well defined. Rights-of-way can be of three types: vehicular routes, drove roads and foot paths. Only the two latter categories are of much relevance in the Western Highlands, and both confer a right of passage for walkers. A drove road also confers right-of-way on horseback, or leading a horse. It is generally considered that a pedal cyclist has the same rights as a pedestrian.

Most Scottish rights-of-way have their origins in the distant past when travel on foot and on horseback was normal, and cattle droving was an important activity. Kirk and coffin roads, leading to churches and graveyards, were also common and led to the establishment of rights-of-way. Briefly, all rights-of-way had their origin in the need by the public to get from place to place in the course of business, pleasure or religious activity.

The essential elements of a public right-of-way are that it should at some time in the past have been in continuous use for a period of not less than twenty years and have been used at any time within the past twenty years, that the use is a matter or right and not due to tolerance on the part of the landowner, that the right-of-way must connect two public places or places to which the public habitually and legitimately resorts, and that it must follow a more or less well defined route. It is not clear if a mountain top can be regarded as a public place, and this would seem to be an important point, because if so then many of our mountains may be considered to have rights-of-way to their summits. As regards the definition of a well defined route, it is not necessary that there should actually be a visible track, rather that it should be established that the public has followed a more or less consistent line during the period in question. Minor deviations such as might be required following the raising of the level of a loch do not invalidate a right-of-way.

For further information the reader is referred to the booklet *Right of Way. A Guide to the Law in Scotland*, published by the Scottish Rights of Way Society Limited, 28 Rutland Square, Edinburgh EH1 2BW.

Maps

No mountaineering guide book can be used by itself, and it is assumed that the reader will also have and know how to use suitable maps for hill-walking. The best map for this purpose is without doubt the Ordnance Survey 1:50,000 maps, both Second Series and Landranger Series, although many will still be using the older One Inch to the Mile maps. This guide book is written on the assumption that its readers will be using the present 1:50,000 maps which are on the whole very accurate and perfectly adequate for route-finding in the mountains. The spelling of place names in this guide book corresponds to that in these maps, and heights are similarly quoted to correspond to those shown on the maps, but there are still some apparent discrepancies which the author has not resolved.

The Ordnance Survey maps of the present Second Series are very up to date, and it is only in a few cases that they have failed to keep pace with changes, particularly the activities of the forest planters. One notable example of this is in Glen Finnan, Glen Pean and Glen Dessarry where there are now newly planted forests with their access roads. There have not been any very recent hydro-electric developments in the Western Highlands, and the Ordnance Survey maps seem to be accurate in respect of enlarged lochs, some of which have considerably changed the glens.

Paths are a problem for the map-maker, and there are instances in current maps where the indication of paths, or the lack of such indication may cause confusion. There are some points in the text where an attempt has been made to clarify matters. Likewise, the showing of footbridges over rivers may not always be accurate, and one must sympathise with the map-makers in their attempts to keep abreast of changes. One example may serve to illustrate this: for many years the map of Knoydart showed a footbridge over the River Carnach near its outflow into Loch Nevis long after the original bridge had collapsed into the river and been swept away, leaving only its end piers. Many walkers must have had a nasty shock to arrive at the river when it was in spate and find it impossible to cross. In 1980 the Knoydart Estate put up a temporary wire bridge, and in 1981 the original bridge was rebuilt. However, the Ordnance Survey, presumably acting on information from some well-meaning individual, deleted the bridge from Sheet 33 in their latest Landranger Series, and so an important error still exists on that map.

Mountain Rescue

In the event of an accident anywhere in the mountains, the standard procedure is that one or more of the injured climber's companions should as quickly as possible telephone the Police (999) who will in turn take the necessary action, including the call-out of a Mountain Rescue Team if required.

There may be a temptation in the event of an accident near the head of Loch Nevis to seek assistance at Camusrory where the Ordnance Survey map shows a Mountain Rescue Post. It must be stressed that, at the time of writing, Camusrory is only occupied intermittently in summer, and the mountain rescue equipment there is not complete, having been subject to vandalism.

Weather

The weather of the Western Highlands is even less reliable than that in other parts of the Scottish Highlands. The rainfall can vary considerably between the western seaboard where the annual average is about 125 cm, and the mountainous watershed 10 or 20 km inland where the annual average is between 300 and 400 cm. Along the Great Glen the figure is about 125 cm. The wettest part of the Western Highlands is around Sgurr na Ciche, in the area between the head of Loch Nevis and Loch Quoich, where the annual average is about 400 cm, and the maximum annual rainfall recorded in recent years was 520 cm at the west end of Loch Quoich, in 1961.

As in most parts of the Highlands, May and June are the best months from the point of view of weather. They are also good months insofar that neither lambing nor stalking are in progress, and there should be no restrictions as regards going onto the hills. At other times of the year August is a notoriously wet month when the majority of days are likely to be wet.

The area is in general rather milder in winter than the rest of the Highlands due to its proximity to the west coast, and good winter climbing conditions are less frequently enjoyed than in the mountains further east.

The foregoing remarks about rainfall should be coupled with a warning about river-crossing. After a spell of wet weather, possibly only a few hours of heavy rain, rivers and burns can rise alarmingly and a stream that in normal circumstances is easy and safe to cross by stepping stones or wading can become impossible, and any attempt to cross may be extremely dangerous. It must therefore be borne in mind that any route through the mountains involving a river crossing where there is no bridge may be foiled by wet weather, and it may be necessary to make a long detour upstream to find a possible crossing place, or one may even have to retreat and wait for the floods to subside.

Hydro-Electric Development

Everyone travelling in the Western Highlands must be aware of the works of the North of Scotland Hydro-Electric Board, and no other part of Scotland has been more affected scenically by the hydro-electric developments of the last 40 years. The high rainfall of the area is one good reason for these developments, and nearly all the major glens have been exploited. While these schemes may have their critics on the grounds of spoiling the natural features and beauty of the glens, and some of the big dams when seen from below are certainly rather stark, on the whole developments have been carried out with respect for the amenities of the area. With the passage of time, the scars of former years have mellowed, and few would now find fault with the work of the Board, provided they do not extend their activities into areas of particularly high scenic and wilderness value.

The Quoich-Garry scheme has involved the enlargement of the two major lochs in Glen Garry. The level of Loch Quoich has been raised to such an extent that a small cut-off dam has also been built at its western end to prevent the waters flooding westwards to Lochan nam Breac and the Carnach River. The Quoich Power Station has a power of 22 MW, and the water flows from it into the enlarged Loch Garry, which now floods much of this glen and supplies the Invergarry Power Station (20 MW) which is situated near the outflow of the River Garry into Loch Oich.

To the north, the Moriston scheme has its major reservoir in Loch

Cluanie, which is topped-up by water from Loch Loyne just to the south. Water from Loch Cluanie flows to the Ceannacroc Power Station (20 MW), and 13 km down Glen Moriston is used again. The River Moriston is dammed below Dundreggan Lodge to form the small and narrow Dundreggan Reservoir, and deep underground below the dam is the Glenmoriston Power Station (36 MW), from which the water flows in a long underground tailrace to Loch Ness near Invermoriston. Livishie is another small scheme (15 MW) which takes its supply from the hills north of Glen Moriston and tops up Dundreggan Reservoir.

The Affric-Beauly scheme has as one of its main reservoirs the greatly enlarged Loch Mullardoch, whose waters flow to Loch Beinn a' Mheadhoin to keep that loch at a more or less constant level, thus avoiding an unsightly 'tide-mark' in beautiful Glen Affric. From Loch Beinn a' Mheadhoin the waters flow to Fasnakyle Power Station (66 MW) and join the River Glass. The other major reservoir of this scheme is Loch Monar at the head of Glen Strathfarrar, which is impounded just below Monar Lodge by a fine double-curvature dam. Deanie (38 MW) and Culligran (24 MW) power stations in Strathfarrar make use of the Loch Monar water before it joins the River Glass at Struy. Lower down Strath Glass two run-of-the-river power stations at Aigas (20 MW) and Kilmorack (20 MW) extract the last of the potential energy of the Affric and Strathfarrar waters before they reach the Beauly Firth.

Another scheme further north, the Conon scheme, has as its catchment area the Fannichs, Strathconon and Glen Orrin. The Luichart (24 MW), Orrin (18 MW) and Torr Achilty (15 MW) power stations form part of this scheme.

Two other small schemes are at Loch Morar, where the large rainfall and catchment area compensate for the very low head, a mere 5 m, to produce 750 kW, and the Nostie Bridge (Lochalsh) scheme where the high head and small catchment area produces 1.25 MW.

Access and Proprietory Rights

Much of the hill country of the Western Highlands is privately owned, and many of these private estates derive much of their revenue from stalking, grouse shooting and fishing, and the renting of sporting rights. Many people living in the Highlands depend on these activities for their livelihood. In addition to these private estates, the Forestry Commission owns vast tracts of land, and other private forestry companies have smaller areas. The National Trust for Scotland have one important mountain property in the Western Highlands, namely Kintail and part of the Inverinate Estate, and access to this area is unrestricted at all times of the year.

As regards privately owned estates, however, it is the policy of the Scottish Mountaineering Club that proprietory, sporting and farming rights should be given due respect at the appropriate seasons of the year. These seasons are: March to May for lambing, August to October for grouse shooting and stalking, and November to January for hind-culling.

At these seasons climbers should seek advice from local shepherds, keepers or stalkers if there is any possibility that their climbing or walking will interfere harmfully with any of these activities. Highland shepherds and keepers are almost invariably courteous and will usually give helpful advice to enable climbers to avoid infringing the legitimate interests of farmers and landowners.

As a guide to those who may wish to contact estate factors in advance to obtain information about access, a list of some known names and addresses of estate factors is given in Appendix III. This information is taken from a document published jointly by the Mountaineering Council of Scotland and the Scottish Landowners Federation in 1981.

It should also be noted that many of the roads in private estates were made and are maintained by the proprietors, who do not acknowledge a public right to motor over them, even though they may follow the lines of established rights-of-way. It may, however, be possible to obtain permission to drive along such private roads if enquiries are made locally.

Geology *by* G. Scott Johnstone

If one stands on any high peak in the Western Highlands (or for that matter in any part of the Highlands of Scotland) the surrounding summits appear to merge in the distance to form a flat horizon. It is easy to appreciate from such a view that the country is not made up of individual mountains thrown up by earth movements such as folding or faulting, but are rather the remnants of a vast, more or less plateau-like upland surface. What appear from below to be separate hills are really the serrated ridges left between the valleys of rivers which are slowly eating into this plateau.

The origins of this Highland Plateau go far back in geological time, but it was essentially formed about 50 million years ago when land started to emerge from the sea over what is now Scotland. As it rose, it formed a broad arch whose axis ran N–S forming a watershed from which rivers flowed in relatively straight courses which trended west or east. These rivers and the waves of the surrounding seas wore down the land mass almost as quickly as it emerged, stripping from it layers of soft sedimentary rock which had been laid down over several geological epochs to lay bare a core of hard, crystalline strata forming the basement to the sedimentary accumulation. This basement proved a rather more formidable adversary to the agents of erosion. Although it, too, was planated to an almost plateau-like surface, it rose more quickly than the seas and rivers could wear it down and now forms the 'High Land' area. Although the present watershed does not necessarily coincide precisely with the original one, the east-and-west flowing rivers have inherited their course from the original drainage pattern and are still doing their best to wear this land away, aided now by a ramifying system of tributaries. The Highland Plateau thus has been dissected into the ridge-mountain systems which we now see. Fortunately for 'Munro baggers', much of the old plateau surface is at or about 3000 ft. above sea level!

Naturally, weak strata are eroded preferentially and one especially weak line was that of the Great Glen of Scotland which follows the line of a great geological fault. This has shattered the rock over a width of half a mile or more, isolating the Western and Northern Highlands (of the S.M.C. classification) from the adjacent Grampian block to the south. There are good geological reasons for believing that along the line of the Great Glen Fault, strata were displaced *laterally* not vertically, this lateral displacement being of the order of 100 km. In other words, what is now the Glen Tarbert area formerly lay opposite Foyers. Some argue for a displacement in the opposite direction.

The hard core of crystalline rocks which make up the Highlands of Scotland belong mainly to the class which the geologist calls metamorphic. That is, they have been metamorphosed (had their form changed) from their original state. In the Western Highlands the strata were originally sandstones or shales (or in places a mixture of alternate laminae of the two types) laid down as sediments in a shallow sea around 900 million years ago. About 500 million years ago, however, these rocks were caught up in a zone of profound crustal movement between two continental masses and subjected to immense pressures,

SKETCH MAP OF THE GEOLOGY OF THE WESTERN HIGHLANDS

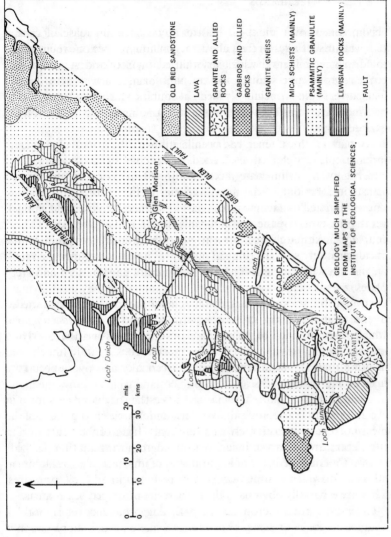

OLD RED SANDSTONE

LAVA

GRANITE AND ALLIED ROCKS

GABBROS AND ALLIED ROCKS

GRANITE GNEISS

MICA SCHISTS (MAINLY)

PSAMMITIC GRANULITE (MAINLY)

LEWISIAN ROCKS (MAINLY)

FAULT

GEOLOGY MUCH SIMPLIFIED FROM MAPS OF THE INSTITUTE OF GEOLOGICAL SCIENCES.

Published by permission of the Director I.G.S., Crown Copyright Reserved

13

accompanied, over most of the area, by a great increase of crustal temperature. As a result their chemical constituents became re-arranged to form new minerals which crystallised in interlocking mosaics to render the rocks very tough and resistant. Sandstones became 'quartz-feldspar-granulites' usually called 'psammitic granulites' and shales became 'mica-schists' or 'pelitic schists'. The laminated rocks became 'striped schists'.

As part of the intense re-crystallisation of the rocks of the area, innumerable tiny clots, threads and lenses of coarse granite were formed which grew in an intimate mixture with the mica-schists and striped schists to form one of the many varieties of the parallel-banded rock known as 'gneiss'. Excess of this coarse granite crystallised out in thick veins criss-crossing the metamorphic strata in all directions. These coarse granites are known as 'pegmatites' and are common in the mica-schist areas. The veins are mainly white or sometimes pale pink and in the white varieties the mineral mica often shows up as silvery plates several inches across.

Deep down below the Western Highlands the metamorphism was so intense that the earth's crust was partially fused to form molten rock which rose upwards to consolidate on cooling within the overlying schists and gneisses as the crystalline igneous rock, granite (much finer in grain than the pegmatite variety). Much more rarely, gabbro rose from even greater depths.

The distribution of these rocks in the Western Highlands is shown in the accompanying geological map. The complex outcrop pattern of the metamorphic rocks is largely as a result of folding of the strata during the metamorphic period. It can be inferred from the map that the folds of this 'Caledonian' episode are in places of immense size, but folds on all scales down to minute puckers can be found in all rock exposures. They are especially obvious in the mica-schist or striped schist areas.

Granulites usually crop out as pale, flaggy-banded yet smoothly-weathering, crags or slabs. Mica-schists make up much more knobbly ground, especially where they are mixed with granite to form gneisses. They are laminated rocks, quite readily split along innumerable parallel parting planes to give lustrous, mica-coated silvery surfaces, although the rock in bulk is dark grey. Granites are massive and smooth weathering, usually pale grey or pale pink in colour, while gabbros of the Caledonian period are very dark in colour although in detail are mottled black and white.

In the extreme tip of the peninsula of Ardnamurchan, however, gabbros and allied rocks of a different age are found. These form part of a great volcanic centre, one of several which were active along the western seaboard and isalnds of Scotland about 60 million years ago, during the Tertiary period (see S.M.C. District Guide, *The Island of Skye*). What is seen in Ardnamurchan is not the old volcano proper, but rather its deep roots, represented by the solidified molten rock which first fed the outpouring lavas and, latterly, rose up to invade the collapsed base of the volcano itself. The structure is incredibly complex in detail, but in general is formed of a series of concentric rings.

Gabbro and the allied rock type, dolerite of Tertiary age commonly weather smooth and massive, but are rough in detail and seamed with cracks which give good holds to the climber. Although the rock is black in colour when fresh, it commonly weathers in shades of rusty brown. Thin parallel sided vertical 'dykes' of dolerite extend well beyond the Tertiary centres and are sparsely distributed in the Western Highlands. In the Morar area, however, they are common, but are not always easy to distinguish from a suite of similar dyke rocks of much earlier (Permian) age which are also of widespread occurrence, especially in the Loch Eil and Morvern areas.

Near Loch Aline are found sparse remnants of the sediments which covered the Highland metamorphic rocks. These are sandstones and shales, mainly of Jurassic age, which have been preserved west of Loch Arienas under a capping of Tertiary lavas which flowed from either the Mull or Ardnamurchan volcanic centres. The white sandstone of Lochaline is mined and crushed to make a glass sand.

Like all of the Highland area of Scotland, the Western Highlands show spectacular evidence of the Glacial Period which commenced perhaps one million, and ended about ten thousand, years ago. At its maximum, a great ice-cap more or less covered the area but what is now most evident are the effects of the last stages of glaciation—the 'valley glacier' period. At that time glaciers, flowing east and west from a median line somewhat east of the present watershed debouched through the main river valleys to the sea on the west and the Great Glen on the east. To start with these valleys probably had the V-shaped cross-section of river erosion, but this was sculptured to a broad U-shape by the action of the glaciers. Near the glacier divide evidence of ice-moulding is readily seen in detail in the bare, glacially-smoothed slabs and small hummocks—the roches moutonnées—which can be found in the valley sides and floors. These latter have a smooth slope facing the glacier impact side and a steep small crag on the pluck, or downstream, side relative to the glacier flow. At higher levels, small glaciers lingered long in the hollows of the hills, eating back into the rock with freeze-thaw action to excavate the cup-shaped corries at the heads of the main and tributary valleys. As they encroached on the ridge tops from either side, so they narrowed them and in places cut through them so that peaks are commonly isolated by depressions with narrow ridge-crests.

It is in the western sea-lochs, however, that the glacier action is most spectacular. Along these long, narrow, fiord-like trenches the upper reaches are often steep and narrow, while the glacier, compressed in these trenches, cut deeply downwards as well as sideways. Loch Morar, for instance, has a depth of about 330 m about one third of the way inland from its seaward end. As the erosive power of the ice declined, either because of widening of the original valley or because the glacier floated on reaching the sea, the glacial overdeepening commonly diminished rapidly towards the end of the fiords, which therefore often have a rock lip near their exits, or at least part-way along their length.

Glacial moraines are almost absent from the western part of the area, but the eastern valleys become clothed in these deposits left by the ice more and more from west to east. In the Great Glen thick sand and gravel deposits washed out from the glacier snouts are seen at the confluence of the side glens with the main valley, where they form relatively fertile flats.

As far as climbing is concerned it must be admitted that the rocks are not well suited to the harder arts of the sport. The area is divided into four main districts, geologically. Referring to the map, the ground east of the mica-schist belt is made up of granulite which tends to occur in flat-lying beds of very even composition so that there are few places where differential erosion can give rise to craggy ground. West of the mica-schist belt the granulites and interbedded mica-schists lie steeply in complex folds and often form cliffs where the rocks, however, tend to be slabby, with vegetatious cracks. Locally as in Kintail some satisfactory climbs are to be found. The big cliffs of Ladhar Bheinn, however, do not seem adapted for good rock-climbing. The main mica-schist belt makes up very rugged ground indeed but, as the rocks are intensely folded on all scales the crags have few continuous lines on them for the climber to follow, while in detail, the rock is rather friable and vegetatious. Where shot through by granite to form gneiss, however, the mica-schist and granulite can supply some fine climbing rock, as at Garbh Bheinn of Ardgour and the hills around Loch Shiel

16

and Glen Dessarry. Unfortunately only in the first area are the crags sufficiently continuous to give good sport.

Of the igneous rocks, the Tertiary complex of Ardnamurchan has good, though short, climbs on gabbro and allied rocks. The granites and earlier gabbros of the area, though potentially good, lack crags. Short climbs on these rocks are mentioned in the appropriate chapter.

Wild Life

The author of this guide book is no naturalist, and the following notes which record some of his observations are supplemented by the notes of G. Scott Johnstone, the author of the previous edition of this guide book.

The red deer is of course the largest and finest of the mammals of our mountains, and they are seen in great numbers throughout the area. They can be a pest to crofters when in winter and spring they descend to low level in search of food in arable land. In summer and autumn they are high in the mountains and corries, but it is not unusual for them to come down to the glens at night to feed on lush riverside grass, and campers may be startled by their appearance at dusk, browsing close to the tents. In spring and early summer the deer may be relatively unafraid at the approach of humans, but in high summer they become much more shy and are disturbed when humans are still some distance away. In autumn the rutting season is in full swing, and the hills resound to the bellowing of the stags, a magnificently wild roaring which echoes from corrie to corrie.

Roe deer are common at lower levels in woodland where they are considered to be a menace because of the damage which they are alleged to do to young trees. When startled they bound away with a sharp dog-like bark.

Wild goats are a magnificent sight with their shaggy coats and great curving horns. They too are rather timid, but one can sometimes get close enough to have a good view of them, and if one is downwind their musty smell is unmistakable. There are herds in many places, for example in Glen Elchaig below Glomach; the north end of the Five Sisters of Kintail; Ardgour, which means goats' peninsula; the head of Loch Morar and the hills south-east of Loch Shiel. Wild goats have their rutting season which is not as noisy as that of the deer, and the males lock horns and wrestle each other. On one occasion the author was able to approach to within a few yards of wild goats engrossed in these struggles.

Foxes are not uncommon, and they can most probably be seen on the snow-covered hills in winter when their red colour gives them no camouflage, and their foot-prints are obvious in the snow. They are actively hunted, and in Ardgour there is a pack of fox-hounds. Badgers, being nocturnal, are only rarely seen by day, and they too are killed by crofters and farmers.

Otters can be seen along the sea-shore and in rivers and inland lochs. Occasionally they may roam some distance from water. Wildcat and pine-marten are rare. Of the small mammals, rats and mice are the ones most likely to be encountered, in bothies. Those who are squeamish about these creatures may have sleepless nights in the bothies as the scurrying of little feet continues all night in search of food. Even if one's supplies are packed in polythene bags and hung from the rafters, there is no certainty that some ingenious little beast will not find a way to help itself.

Seals are common round the shore line, and can often be seen. Those in canoes or dinghies have the best chance of an encounter among off-shore skerries and around 'seal-islands', such as one near the head of Loch Nevis.

Of the many birds to be seen, the golden eagle is the one which causes greatest excitement. It is not by any means uncommon in the Western Highlands, but it may be difficult to distinguish the golden eagle from the buzzard unless one is close enough to be certain of the much greater size of the former. The eagle has a more soaring flight, and the buzzard (which is far more common) may give itself away by its plaintive mewing cry. The raven is another fine bird of the high mountains and crags which is easily recognised by its all black plumage and characteristic croak.

Other rarer birds of prey that may be seen in the mountains include the peregrine falcon with its fast aerobatic flight, and (much rarer) the osprey which is slowly re-establishing itself in Scotland and may be seen in the Western Highlands.

Along the loch-side and sea-shore the heron is a familiar sight, wading in shallow water or just standing still waiting for its prey to appear, and be snapped up. Heronries may be on small islets (as in Loch Hourn) or in woodland some little distance from the water's edge, and the nests are untidy bundles of twigs among the tree tops.

Black- and red-throated divers may be seen on remote hill-lochs where they nest. Many of the common waders are seen and heard. For example, the plaintive cry of the golden plover on the hills and upland moors is usually heard some time before the bird is seen. The common snipe is likely to stay put in the heather until one is almost on top of it, and only then does it take off in its erratic high-speed flight. It can often be identified by the drumming sound which it makes when diving in flight. Oystercatcher, curlew, ringed plover and sandpiper are all common.

Of the smaller birds, the dipper is a familiar sight along streams, flying close to the water and perching on boulders. The ring ouzel (or mountain blackbird) is often seen on hillsides perched on crags and rocks. The wheatear is a common sight, easily identified by its white rumps as it flies away, and the stonechat is a colourful and rather noisy bird that frequents rough moorland, perching on top of clumps of heather or gorse.

The red grouse is not nearly as common on the western mountains as it is in the central or eastern highlands. The ptarmigan, however, is quite commonly seen high on the mountains despite its plumage which gives it good camouflage. It is quite possible to get close to these birds for they seem reluctant to fly off until the climber is only a few yards away; then they skim off with their familiar croaky call. Blackcock (or black grouse) may be seen, but their habitat does not extend far west of the Great Glen.

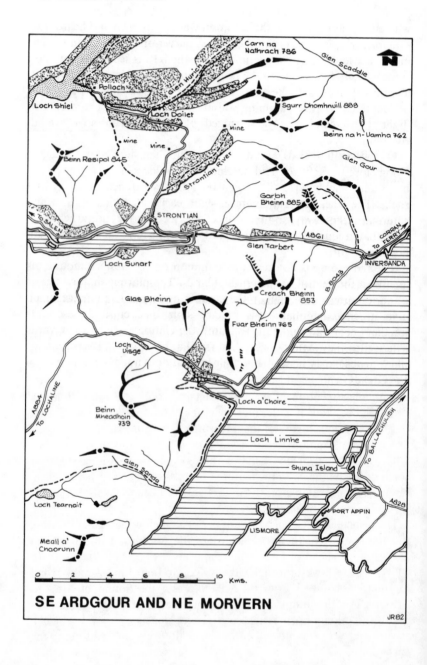

SE ARDGOUR AND NE MORVERN

1

Morvern

Creach Bheinn (853 m) 871577
Fuar Bheinn (765 m) 853563
Beinn na Cille (651 m) 854542
Beinn Mheadhoin (739 m) 799514
Sithean na Raplaich (550 m) 636517
Beinn Iadain (571 m) 692561

MAPS: Ordnance Survey 1:50,000 Sheets 40, 47 and 49.

Morvern is the southernmost district of the Western Highlands, and it is almost entirely surrounded by the sea, being joined to Ardgour only at its north-east corner where Glen Tarbert slices through the hills between Loch Linnhe and the head of Loch Sunart. The name Morvern is derived from A'Mhorbhairn, which means the sea-gap, and refers to the Sound of Mull which, with Loch Sunart and Loch Linnhe, forms the coastal perimeter of Morvern.

With the exception of its north-eastern corner, Morvern is not a mountainous land. For the most part it is high undulating moorland and rounded hills, many of them featureless and in places very boggy. The Forestry Commission own much of the land, and there are some extensive forested areas. Some of these, such as the Fiunary Forest north of Lochaline, are now mature and in the process of being felled. Elsewhere, for example on the moors east of Gleann Geal, the forests are quite recently planted.

The principal village of Morvern is Lochaline on the Sound of Mull, and the main road there (A884) leaves the A861 road through Glen Tarbert at the head of Loch Sunart and more or less bisects Morvern on its way south-west through Gleann Geal to Lochaline. A minor road continues north-west from the village along the Sound of Mull to Drimnin. Another minor road leaves the A884 near Claggan and goes north-west along Loch Arienas to Kinlochteacuis, beyond which a private and very rough road continues to Rahoy. The road along the north coast of Morvern to Glencripesdale is private, and a gate across

c

it near its eastern end is usually locked. Finally, there is a narrow road from Inversanda in the north-east corner of Morvern going south-west to Kingairloch, and then west to join the A884. At one point along the side of Loch Linnhe this road is quite spectacular, with the hillside rising very steeply in red cliffs on one side, and the sea pounding against the retaining wall on the other. It is this road that gives access to the most mountainous corner of Morvern.

Lochaline is the one place in Morvern where the visiting climber or walker is likely to find accommodation and refreshment. It is not a particularly attractive village, but the car ferry to Mull sails from there, so at times there is an air of activity about the place. Lochaline's main claim to fame is the sand mine whose tunnels run for a considerable distance underground, beneath the village. The sand is of a very pure quality, suitable for optical glass. It was first mined in 1939, and the deposits have been worked ever since then, providing Morvern with one of its main sources of employment, the other being forestry.

At the time of writing there are plans to develop a super-quarry to extract granite at the foot of Glen Sanda on the Loch Linnhe shore of Morvern, facing Lismore. This spot is very remote, with no road access (the granite will be shipped out in large bulk carriers) and the visual effect will be seen only by sailors in the Lynn of Morvern.

Among several points of interest in Morvern that might be visited on an off-day, mention may be made of a few. Ardtornish Castle on a peninsula south-east of Loch Aline was the stronghold of the Lords of the Isles in the fourteenth and fifteenth centuries, and later of MacLean of Duart. Now little remains of this dark fortress; it can be reached along the east side of Loch Aline, or possibly by boat across the narrows at the mouth of the loch. Ardtornish Point, on which the castle stands, commands a fine view in both directions along the Sound of Mull. At the head of Loch Aline stands Kinlochaline Castle on a crag above the loch. This square keep was once the seat of the chiefs of Clan MacInnes, but it was stormed and burned by Cromwellian troops in the seventeenth century. It was restored in 1890, and anyone wishing to visit the castle should enquire at the nearby cottage where the key is kept.

Not far up the River Aline are the cottages of Larachbeg where the folk from St. Kilda were settled in 1930 after they left their native island. Some of the men worked in the Fiunary Forest nearby. The road from Claggan (1 km north of Larachbeg) to Kinlochteacuis is pleasantly quiet, and gives some good views of the north side of Sithean na

Raplaich whose steeply planted hillside and crowning escarpment give this hill a fine appearance. Just beyond the end of the public road one comes to Kinloch where there is a deer farming experiment in progress, and one can see deer grazing in the fields at the head of Loch Teacuis. Continuing on foot along the private road on the north-east side of the loch for a further 3 km one comes to the dun of Rahoy, a vitrified fort on a knoll overlooking the narrow entrance to Loch Teacuis. The name Rahoy is derived from 'rath thuaith', the north fort, and the dun was excavated by Professor Childe in 1936–37.

Creach Bheinn (853 m), **Fuar Bheinn** (765 m), **Beinn na Cille** (651 m)

Turning now to the mountains of Morvern, Creach Bheinn is the highest, and with its neighbours Fuar Bheinn, Maol Odhar (c.786 m) and Beinn na Cille it forms the most important, some might say the only important group in the district. Certainly the finest day's hill-walking in Morvern is the traverse of these hills along the skyline enclosing Glen Galmadale.

The start may be made near Camasnacroise and Beinn na Cille is climbed by its south ridge which is grassy with outcropping granite. The map indicates a number of steep little corries on the east side of the ridge to Fuar Bheinn, but they are not particularly interesting or impressive, and the ridge itself is broad as it rises to Fuar Bheinn and continues across the featureless col, the Cul Mham, to Creach Bheinn. There is a fairly large cairn on this summit, which commands a fine view, particularly southwards to the Firth of Lorne. A short distance north-east of the summit, at a slight dip in the ridge, there is a substantial dry stone walled enclosure, rather like a primitive fortifica-tion, but probably a look-out post which is reputed to have been built on the mountain in the time of the Napoleonic wars. Continuing north-east, the ridge is now narrower with steep corries on both sides, and the rounded top of Maol Odhar is reached. There the ridge turns south and continues undulating over Meall nan Each and down the Druim na Maodalaich. The east side of this ridge drops precipitously into Loch Linnhe in broken cliffs of red granite cut by innumerable basalt dykes which form gullies and chimneys lined with trees and bushes, but useless for climbing. The descent of this ridge brings one to the foot of Glen Galmadale barely a kilometre from the day's starting point.

There is a path for some distance up Glen Galmadale, at whose head the south face of Creach Bheinn rises steeply in scree slopes and minor crags; not a recommended route of ascent. The grassy ridge south of Maol Odhar is a better route of ascent and descent at the head of this glen.

The shortest ascent of Creach Bheinn, however, is from the north, leaving the road in Glen Tarbert about 6 km east of Strontian and climbing the Choire Dhuibh. The western side of this corrie and its headwall are quite steep and rocky, but an easy route can be made up the east side onto Maol Odhar before turning west to Creach Bheinn. The broad ridge bounding Choire Dhuibh on the west is also a quick route, but further west the hillside is featureless and uninteresting.

Beinn Mheadhoin (739 m)

To the south of these hills, on the opposite side of Loch a' Choire, is Beinn Mheadhoin. This hill has some fine corries on its north-east side overlooking Kingairloch House, but the south-west side is feature-less moorland above Gleann Geal. The most direct ascent of Beinn Mheadhoin is up the prominent ridge rising above the Old Mill in Corry directly to the summit. Alternatively, one might go up Coire Ban where there is a path for some distance. Once on the summit of Beinn Mheadhoin, if the weather is fine, one should continue the traverse south-east along the ridge to the col at Lag a' Mhaim and then descend to the head of Loch a' Choire by one of the ridges which enclose Coire Reidh. (In view of the fact that the approach just described goes through the grounds of Kingairloch House, it would be advisable to seek permission). An alternative route to Beinn Mheadhoin starts on the B8043 road near the outflow from Loch Uisge and goes up Coire Shalachain and over the flat top of Meall na Greine.

Sithean na Raplaich (550 m), Beinn Iadain (571 m)

Sithean na Raplaich is the highest point of the extensive Fiunary Forest north-west of Lochaline. The finest feature of the hill is the long escarpment of volcanic rock along its north-east face overlooking Loch Arienas. This escarpment and the densely planted forest along the hillside below it form a very effective barrier against any ascent of the hill from the north-east. The only possibility known to the author of a route from Loch Arienas is to take the forest road from Camas Allt a' Choire up into An Coire and scramble up a rather steep slope to the

Dubh Bhealach from where a pleasant walk along the grassy ridge leads to the top. However, tree-felling is in progress at the time of writing, and this access route may alter. (Enquiries at the Loch Aline Forest Office may elicit some useful information about access routes). An alternative ascent, which is shorter and circumvents both forest and escarpment, starts on the road to Kinlochteacuis at the south-east end of Loch Doire nam Mart. Negotiate some rather boggy ground low down and climb westwards on the north side of the forest to reach the shoulder of Sithean na Raplaich north-east of the summit.

Beinn Iadain is the highest hill north of Loch Arienas, an area which can best be described as undulating moorland. The shortest ascent is from Kinloch at the head of Loch Teacuis, following the Kinloch River and Coire an Tuim to the flat boggy ridge north-west of the hill. The final climb up the narrowing north-west ridge is much more interesting over the beds of outcropping lava which are a distinctive feature of this hill. The alternative approach from the south is longer and leads over very boggy ground at the head of the Arienas Burn; so boggy that the Ordnance Survey map describes the area as Lochan Beinn Iadain.

There is a good cross-country walk from Kinlochteacuis round the northern tip of Morvern to Liddesdale on the A884 road. The path northwards from Kinloch crosses the Bealach Sloc an Eich, from where Beinn Ghormaig is only a short climb, and continues down through the forest to Glencripesdale. From there a long walk along the private road on the south shore of Loch Sunart leads eventually to Liddesdale (21 km).

2

Ardnamurchan

Ben Hiant (528 m) 537632
Beinn na Seilg (342 m) 456642
Meall nan Con (437 m) 504682
Ben Laga (512 m) 645622

MAPS: Ordnance Survey 1:50,000 (2nd Series) Sheets 40, 47.

Ardnamurchan is the long peninsula which extends 28 km westwards from Salen and Acharacle to the Point of Ardnamurchan, the western-most tip of the British mainland. It is not a mountainous district, being for the most part rough undulating moorland which only occasionally rises high and steeply enough to form recognisable hills. The charm of Ardnamurchan lies in its remoteness (for it is reached by a narrow and twisting road) and its fine coastline which in some places shows wild rocky cliffs and in others placid sandy bays. For climbers there are a few hills of modest height and some small crags, however they all have a fine character for the crags are of rough gabbro and the hills command wide and spacious views of the western seaboard. This is a region which will be visited more for the feeling of peace and relaxation that it gives rather than the rigours of its climbing.

If one excepts the ferry service between Tobermory on the Island of Mull and Kilchoan, the only route of access to Ardnamurchan is the narrow twisting B8007 road which goes westwards from Salen along the north shore of Loch Sunart and eventually reaches almost to the Point of Ardnamurchan. Fortunately for the climber this road passes close to most of the hills of interest. Accommodation in Ardnamurchan is available in the four main villages—Acharacle, Salen, Glenborrodale and Kilchoan, and in numerous cottages offering bed and breakfast and caravans to let. Camping is not altogether easy as campers seem to be unwelcome at some of the most attractive places such as Sanna or Portuairk.

The eastern half of Ardnamurchan is metamorphic rock, and the hills and moors are typical of the Highlands, rough and craggy. Ben Laga (512 m) is the highest hill in this area, and its steep rocky face above

Loch Sunart is defended along most of its lower edge by a fairly impenetrable mixture of deep heather and trees. At Laga on the south-west side of the summit there is a track leading from the road up onto the open hillside, and this is probably the best way to start the ascent of this hill.

Further west, beyond Loch Mudle, the geology is quite different, and so is the scenery. The rock is principally gabbro, the region having once been the site of a great volcano. The last vent of this volcano can be identified as a rather insignificant little hump midway between Achnaha and Glendrian, 6 km north-north-west of Kilchoan. This knoll is at the centre of a plain about 4 km in diameter surrounded on all sides except one by low gabbro hills, the only gap in this ring being the valley of the Allt Sanna on the north-west.

There is a good deal of bare rock in the western half of Ardnamurchan, and the hills, which are mostly grassy on their lower slopes, have gabbro outcrops along their crests, and on one or two of them, notably Meall nan Con and Beinn na Seilg, there are crags which are big and steep enough to give some climbing.

Mingarry Castle, 1½ km south-east of Kilchoan, is a fine ruined keep on the cliff-edge above the Sound of Mull. Its origins in the thirteenth century are obscure, but for two or three centuries it was a stronghold of the MacIains of Ardnamurchan, Lords of the Isles. At the end of the fifteenth century James IV visited the castle twice to receive the allegiance of the island chiefs, and a hundred years later the castle withstood a siege by Spanish soldiers, hence the name Port nan Spainteach for the little bay below the castle. In 1644 Colkitto MacDonald, in support of Charles I and Montrose, took the castle from the Campbells who were then in possession, and withstood a siege by Argyll's army, but the Campbells regained possession and were in Mingarry at the time of the 1745 rising.

Sanna Bay at the end of one of the roads beyond Kilchoan is the most popular spot in Ardnamurchan by virtue of its fine sandy beaches. Two kilometres south-west the smaller bay at Port na Cairidh is also well worth a vist, and the little hill Sgurr nam Meann which rises above it has a steep cliff just below its summit and might be worth a visit with a rope if one is camping by the bay.

Ben Hiant (528 m), **Meall nan Con** (437 m), **Beinn na Seilg** (342 m)

Ben Hiant, the holy mountain, is the highest hill in Ardnamurchan and, in the writer's opinion, is the one which must be climbed for its view if nothing else. The southern side rises steeply from the Sound of Mull, the lowest precipitous slopes forming the bold headland called Maclean's Nose. To the north of the summit there is a steep basalt buttress below which grassy corries drop gently to the flat moorland recently covered by forest plantation.

The shortest and most pleasant ascent of Ben Hiant is from the road about $1\frac{1}{2}$ km north-east of the summit. After the first short steep climb one reaches a grassy ridge forming a fine escarpment to the south-east, and the walk up this undulating ridge is delightful, with a final short steep climb to the top. The ascent from the west is longer and involves crossing cultivated land east of the Allt Choire Mhuilinn; there is a good deal of cattle grazing on the moors north-west of Ben Hiant. One can, however, follow a recently made track which leads across these moors on the north of Beinn na h-Urchrach where the footpath shown on the OS map is joined, and the final ascent of Ben Hiant can be made up its north-west shoulder.

As a viewpoint, the summit of Ben Hiant has no equal in Ardnamurchan. To the east there are fine views up Loch Sunart and into the lonely recesses of Loch Teacuis backed by the hills of Morvern. In the distance are the higher hills of Sunart and Ardgour. Turning round, there is a panorama of the western seaboard from the Sound of Mull to the Sound of Sleat, with the islands of the Hebrides along the horizon.

Meall nan Con is the highest of half a dozen gabbro topped hills in the western half of Ardnamurchan, and there are some crags on its west side that give it some interest. High up near the summit there is a cliff overlooking a tiny unnamed lochan. The central and longest buttress, a mere 50 m high, gives a pleasant Very Difficult climb, and the steep little crag to its south, composed of very rough gabbro, gives several climbs of 15 to 20 m length, and Very Difficult and harder standard. Some distance further west, at Map Reference 492678, there is another gabbro cliff which according to C. Stead is about 100 m high and has several routes of Very Difficult to Severe standard. The shortest approach to this cliff is from the road between Kilchoan and Sanna, $1\frac{1}{2}$ km south-east of Achnaha, whereas the shortest approach to the summit of Meall nan Con is from the road junction 3 km south-east of the hill. C. Stead has also reported rock-climbing on the knoll of Meall an Fhir-eoin, $2\frac{1}{2}$ km north-west of Meall nan Con.

The westernmost 300 m hill in Ardnamurchan is Beinn na Seilg, which rises above the rough moorland 3 km west of Kilchoan. There is a lot of bare gabbro on this little hill, and the north peak in particular has a fine crag on its west side. The ascent can be made easily from almost any point to the east of the hill. For example, one can start from Ormsaig, leaving the road about 1 km beyond its junction on the west edge of Kilchoan, and climbing the grassy hillside north-westwards past the Lochain Ghleann Locha. The moorland on the north-east side of the hill is rather rough going over heather and peat bog, but the shortest approach to the crags on the west face of the north peak starts from the road at Lochan na Crannaig and goes south-west across this moor. The view from Beinn na Seilg is very fine, some might say even finer than that from Ben Hiant. Certainly the outlook westwards is quite uninterrupted by any other hills.

The cliff on the west side of the north peak was first explored by R. E. Chapman and G. Francis in 1949, and they climbed six routes. Since then there has doubtless been further exploration, but no further routes have been recorded. The cliff is broken near its north end by an area of broken rocks and grass; the part to the north of this Central Break is *Cuillin Buttress*, and the larger crag to the south is *Hebrides Wall*. The rock is good rough gabbro. Route descriptions are as follows:—

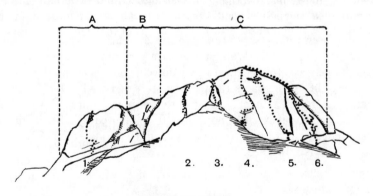

BEINN NA SEILG

A. Cuillin Buttress	B. Central Break	C. Hebrides Wall
1. Sunset Wall	3. Gabbro Slab	5. Faradh Dubh
2. Geologist's Groove	4. Trident Climb	6. South-West Buttress

1. *Sunset Wall* (45 m, Very Difficult). Start near the centre of Cuillin Buttress below two prominent grass ledges. Climb inclined ledges to a

grass ledge, traverse left and up steep rocks to a pulpit and finally up a slab on the right.

2. *Geologist's Groove* (30 m, Difficult). Start mid-way between the Central Break and Gabbro Slab. Climb a heather filled crack until an overhang forces a move left; return right to a wide bay and continue up the crack to easy rocks.

3. *Gabbro Slab* (15 m, Moderate). Climb the rough slab from the highest point of the grass below the crag.

4. *Trident Climb* (40 m, Very Difficult). The climb is named after a three-pronged flake of rock a short distance to the right of and below Gabbro Slab. Climb the prongs and stand on a rather loose block jammed behind the topmost one. Make a long stride to the right and pull up onto a roomy ledge; make a rising traverse to the right to reach a thin crack and climb this to a ledge and easier ground.

5. *Faradh Dubh* (55 m, Very Difficult). Start at a cairn just left of the prominent steep crack on the right side of Hebrides Wall. Climb steeply up to the left and then straight up to two rounded bulges. (Belay). Either traverse left to avoid the bulges or climb directly over the right hand one to reach an overhang. Traverse left until the overhang can be surmounted, and easy ground is reached.

6. *South-west Buttress* (50 m, Moderate). This is the right-hand boundary of Hebrides Wall, and gives a pleasant scramble on good rock if one keeps to the left. An easy descent route is round the corner on the right. A few paces right of the start of Faradh Dubh a cairn marks the start of a direct alternative to South-west Buttress. A vertical wall is climbed on excellent holds for 10 m, followed by a Severe move on rounded holds to reach easier rocks and the normal route. (S.M.C.J., Vol. XXIV, No. 141, p. 229).

Walks and Paths

At the western tip of Ardnamurchan there is pleasant coastal walking between Sanna and the Point, passing the tiny village at Portuairk.

Kilmory to Arivegaig. This is a good walk, which probably requires two cars to be feasible, along the north side of Ardnamurchan. There are fine views to the Inner Hebrides. The first 3 km from Kilmory follow the road east to Ockle farm, and the continuation is by a track over the shoulder of Beinn Bhreac and down to the fine sandy bay at Gortenfern. The last part of the walk is through forestry plantation and along the edge of Kentra Bay to Arevigaig where the public road is reached (15 km).

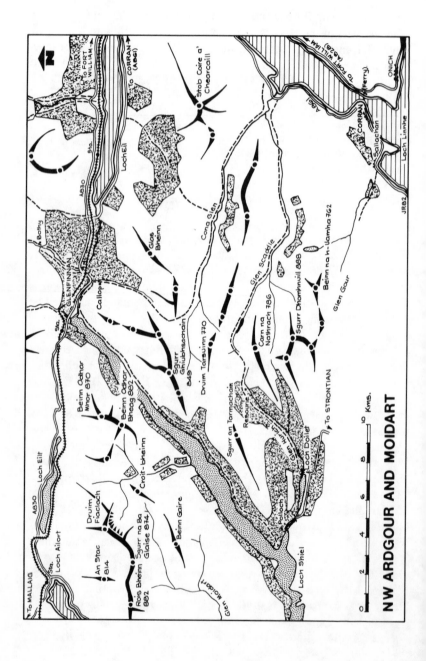

NW ARDGOUR AND MOIDART

3

Ardgour and Sunart

Garbh Bheinn (885 m) 903622
Sgurr Dhomhnuill (888 m) 890679
Sgurr Ghiubhsachain (849 m) 875751
Beinn Resipol (845 m) 767655

MAPS: Ordnance Survey 1:50,000 (2nd Series) Sheets 40 and 41.

These two districts of the Western Highlands lie to the west of Loch
Linnhe, across the narrows at Corran, and the grand outline of the
Ardgour mountains as seen from Ballachulish or Onich gives this
region a special character. For the traveller coming north-westwards
through Scotland, the first view of the Western Highlands may well be
the view of these mountains, and it is unforgettable.

The two districts of Ardgour and Sunart are bounded by four lochs—
Linnhe, Eil, Shiel and Sunart—and the low-lying glens which connect
them. So low is the watershed between Loch Eil and Loch Shiel,
less than 20 m above sea-level, that Ardgour, Sunart, Morvern and
Ardnamurchan almost form a large offshore island of complex shape.
These districts seem to have as many characteristics of the Scottish
islands as of the mainland.

It is in Ardgour that we first see the typical east-west 'grain' of the
Western Highlands. Glen Tarbert, Glen Gour, Glen Scaddle, the Cona
Glen and Loch Eil all show this characteristic feature. Between these
valleys there are some very rugged ridges which culminate in three
outstanding mountains—Garbh Bheinn, Sgurr Dhomhnuill and Sgurr
Ghiubhsachain. Ardgour as a whole is a very wild and mountainous
district, and only in the Strontian Glen and at Loch Doilet, where there
is a Forestry Commission village at Polloch, are there any habitations
more than a kilometre or two from its perimeter. The boundary
between Ardgour and Sunart is the pass between Strontian and Loch
Doilet, and Sunart itself is quite a small district completely dominated
by a single mountain, Beinn Resipol.

Access to three sides of the area described in this chapter is easy, for the A861 road goes along the south side of Loch Eil, the west side of Loch Linnhe as far south as Inversanda and from there westwards through Glen Tarbert and along the north shore of Loch Sunart. On the fourth side, along Loch Shiel, access by car is not possible for the Forestry Commission road along the south-east side of the loch is private. (The gate across this road at its north-east end where it crosses the River Callop is normally locked, however there seems to be no reason why one should not cycle along the road). The circuit of Ardgour is completed by the hill road which connects Strontian with Polloch. This road climbs steeply past abandoned mine workings to cross the pass at 342 m and descend even more steeply through the forest to Loch Doilet and Polloch, where the public road ends.

For visiting walkers and climbers there are several centres from which the area can be explored. Probably the best is Strontian, an attractive village near the head of Loch Sunart which is a very good base for exploring the whole of this southern part of the Western Highlands, Morvern and Ardnamurchan included. There are shops, hotels, chalets, camping and caravan sites, in fact just about everything a visitor to the Western Highlands can expect to find. Acharacle at the foot of Loch Shiel is another good centre with hotels, shops, bed and breakfast accommodation and the possibility of hiring dinghies on Loch Shiel. There are hotels at Salen, Ardgour village and Glenfinnan near the north-west corner of Ardgour, and elsewhere there are, in season, innumerable cottages offering bed and breakfast, and good sites for wild camping abound. One bothy in the area described in this chapter may also be mentioned; it is Resourie, a little cottage 6 km up Glen Hurich from the head of Loch Doilet in a wild and remote part of Ardgour.

For those without their own transport, access to Strontian, Salen and Acharacle must be by bus: first from Fort William to Corran, then across the ferry and finally by the once-a-day service from Ardgour village to Kilchoan in Ardnamurchan. On the north side of Ardgour there is the railway from Fort William to Mallaig, and finally there is a passenger ferry from Fort William to Camusnagaul on the north-east corner of Ardgour.

Strontian is well known for the lead mines on the hillside north of the village, and the road to Loch Doilet passes several old shafts, some of which can be explored at one's own risk. These mines date from 1722, and ceased production in 1904. The old mine dumps and shafts contain a wide variety of interesting minerals; probably the most attractive are the crystals of galena (lead sulphide) which when broken have a silvery lustre. In 1764 the mineral strontianite was first found in these mines, and from it the element strontium was discovered for the first time. There are signs that the mines may now be worked again.

Garbh Bheinn (885 m)

Garbh Bheinn, situated in the south-east corner of Ardgour, is the finest mountain in this district, and arguably one of the half dozen grandest in the Western Highlands. From the rock-climber's point of view it is certainly the finest, for it has more good rock than any other West Highland peak. The fine outline of Garbh Bheinn when seen from afar has already been mentioned, and this distant impression of bold rock ridges, buttresses and gullies is confirmed at close quarters. The chief glory of the mountain is its rocky east face rising above the head of Coire an Iubhair. One has to walk 3 km up this corrie by quite a good stalker's path before the face is revealed, and it is a great sight: on the left, dropping directly below the summit, is the 300 m high Great Ridge, with the dark gash of the Great Gully on its right; further right are the towers of the Pinnacle Ridge, and to the right again are the slabby rocks of the North-East and North buttresses.

Garbh Bheinn is well named the rough mountain, for it has a lot of rough bare rock, a grey quartzo-felspathic gneiss, not only on its east face, but on all its flanks. There is a subsidiary top a few hundred metres west of the summit, and $\frac{1}{2}$ km south-east is the top of Sron a' Gharbh Choire Bhig (810 m) from which a long ridge continues south-eastwards, its slabby north-east face overlooking Coire an Iubhair. Northwards from the summit of Garbh Bheinn a broad rocky ridge goes over the top of the Pinnacle Ridge and the North-East Buttress (marked by a small quartzite cairn) to the top of the north face which drops steeply to Lochan Coire an Iubhair.

Garbh Bheinn is most frequently climbed from the south or south-east, and there are at least four distinct routes, each with their own character. The shortest, but least aesthetic route is up the Coire a' Chothruim (unnamed on the Ordnance Survey map) which is south of the summit. The distance to the summit from the road at the watershed of Glen Tarbert is about 2 km and the ascent is continuously steep and stony, and its only merit would seem to be its directness.

For the next three routes the starting point is at the foot of Coire an Iubhair, and cars can be parked off the road near the old bridge. There

35

are good camp sites nearby, and climbers are asked to request camping permission at Inversanda House. A fine route of ascent is up the long Sron a' Gharbh Choire Bhig ridge; there is a tenuous path for much of the way which starts about a 100 m west of the bridge just mentioned. From the summit of the Sron there is a grand view across the intervening corrie to the summit of Garbh Bheinn and the tremendous south face of the Great Ridge which drops directly below it. The final part of this route goes up easy rocky slopes west of this face, and gives a good view of its steepness.

A third route goes up the Coire an Iubhair by the well worn, but often muddy path on the east side of the stream. This is the rock-climbers' trade route, and leads to the foot of the east face. At the point where the streams meet the left hand (south) one is followed steeply upwards by a faint path below the slabby lower rocks of the Great Ridge to reach the col between Sron a' Gharbh Choire Bhig and Garbh Bheinn, and the previous route is joined.

The circuit of Coire an Iubhair is a very fine expedition, and it gives magnificent views of Garbh Bheinn as well the interesting ascent of its north face. The best way to do the traverse is anti-clockwise, starting up the east side of the corrie along Druim an Iubhair and continuing over Sgorr Mhic Eacharna to Beinn Bheag (730 m). One kilometre further west, after crossing a lower top of Beinn Bheag, one reaches the top of a steep scree and grass gully which leads down to Lochan Coire an Iubhair which is beautifully situated in the Bealach Feith'n Amean. From the lochan the north face of Garbh Bheinn rises very steeply, the rocky North Face buttress on the left and a straight narrow gully on the right. In between there is a steep slope of mixed rock and grass which is an easy scramble in summer. In winter, however, the gully is probably a better route for although it is quite steep, it has no pitches. Above this one scrambles up superbly rough and easy-angled rock to reach the little quartzite cairn at the top of North-East Buttress, and so to the summit. The descent by the Sron a' Gharbh Choire Bhig ridge completes a superb traverse, undoubtedly the best in Ardgour.

Rock Climbs on Garbh Bheinn

As already mentioned, the rock-climbing on the east face of Garbh Bheinn is the best in the Western Highlands. The rock is a superb rough grey gneiss, often contorted to form pockets and flakes which make excellent holds. There are some bands of quartzite rocks here and there

1. *Looking across the Lynn of Morvern from Lismore towards Creach Bheinn.*

2. *Garbh Bheinn from the north-east.*

3. The north-east face of Garbh Bheinn above the head of Coire an Iubhair.

4. Looking across Loch Linnhe towards the Ardgour mountains, with Garbh Bheinn rising above the nearer ridge of Druim an Iubhair.

5. *Looking south from the ridge of Beinn Bheag towards Garbh Bheinn.*

6. *The summit of Garbh Bheinn from the south-east. The south face of the Great Ridge is in sunshine.*

7.   On the Great Ridge of Garbh Bheinn.

8. *The North-East Buttress of Garbh Bheinn.*

9. *On Route Two of the North-East Buttress, Garbh Bheinn.*

10. Loch Doilet in the Glenhurich Forest; the two peaks are Carn na Nathrach (left) and Druim Garbh (right).

11. Resourie Bothy at the head of Glen Hurich in the wilds of Ardgour.

which are smooth and polished in contrast to the rough gneiss. When wet, the rock is as slippery as on most Scottish mountains, and this remark is particularly apt to the quartzite which becomes positively treacherous. The upper part of Coire an Iubhair has some splendid features; ridges, buttresses, slabs and gullies, which give a great variety of climbs, many of them leading up to the summit ridge of Garbh Bheinn. It is beyond the scope of this guidebook to give details of all existing climbs on the mountain, and for this the reader is referred to the Scottish Mountaineering Club's *Guide to Rock and Ice Climbs in Lochaber and Badenoch*, by A. C. Stead and J. R. Marshall. This is a selective guide, and all the best routes on Garbh Bheinn are described.

Standing below the east face in the upper part of Coire an Iubhair one can get a good impression of the cliffs. The small subsidiary corrie on the left (south) is the Garbh Choire Mor, and at its head is the col between Sron a' Gharbh Choire Bhig and Garbh Bheinn. On the south side of this little corrie there is a large expanse of crags, slabs and minor buttresses on the flank of Sron a' Gharbh Choire Bhig. The largest crag, situated low down, is the Leac Beag Buttress, whose identifying feature is a large grey slab topped by an overhanging belt of rock. The buttress is divided into two wings by a central vegetated groove. *Dexter* (140 m, Severe) by L. S. Lovat and C. Ford is a pleasant route with good situations up the right-hand edge of the right wing. Some 250 m west and slightly above the Leac Beag Buttress is Garbh Choire Buttress on which there are at least four routes of Severe and Very Severe standard, up to 100 m long. Further up the corrie, not far below the col, are the Garbh Choire Slabs which can be climbed almost anywhere at Very Difficult to Severe standard.

Just below and to the right of the col at the head of the Garbh Choire Mor is *Bealach Buttress*. The route on this buttress starts at the lowest rocks and follows the line of least resistance to the left-hand of two narrow arêtes which leads to the top (110 m, Very Difficult), D. D. Stewart and D. N. Mill.

The finest feature of Garbh Bheinn is the *Great Ridge* which rises steeply for over 300 m on the right-hand side of the Garbh Choire Mor to the summit of the mountain. The lowest part of the ridge is a broad apron of steep slabs which in places overhang around their base. Higher up the buttress narrows and forms a well-defined ridge soaring up to the summit. The ridge was first ascended by J. H. Bell and W. Brown in 1897, and since then it has become the classic climb on Garbh Bheinn. The lower belt of steep slabs was bypassed on the first ascent, which started up the ridge at the point where it becomes a narrow and well-defined arête above a broad grassy ledge which crosses the buttress. This point can be reached either by steep slabs and grass on the north side (above Great Gully), or more easily by climbing the open slabby gully on the left of the base of the Great Ridge until it is possible to traverse right, out of the gully and across the broad grass ledge to reach the foot of the ridge proper. The start of the ridge is a narrow rock arête and a short steep corner. Thereafter the climb continues close to the crest on excellent rock with splendid situations, and gradually the climbing becomes easier as one nears the summit (250 m, Difficult). The *Direct Start* to the *Great Ridge* makes a good hard introduction by ascending the lower slabs directly. One route is up the prominent steep crack with dark overhanging rocks on its left and pale slabs on the right. After 25 m the route emerges onto more open rock and fine rough slabs are climbed. An alternative start is by steep slabs to the right of the prominent crack. Both variations converge at an obvious chimney formed by a large detached flake, and above this the grass ledge is reached at which the original route starts. The *Great Ridge* with *Direct Start* was first climbed by D. D. Stewart and D. N. Mill, and is a very fine route (350 m, Very Difficult).

The South Wall of Great Ridge is a magnificent steep wall directly below the summit of Garbh Bheinn. There are two tiers separated by a terrace. The wall has several first class routes of between 50 and 110 m, all very steep and exposed, on excellent rock and between Very Difficult and Very Severe is standard. The original route, *Scimitar* (105 m, Very Severe) was climbed in 1952 by D. D. Stewart and D. N. Mill, and since then several of Scotland's leading climbers have added their contributions to the cliff. Probably the classic route is *Butterknife* (105 m, Severe) by J. R. Marshall, A. H. Hendry, G. J. Ritchie and I. D. Haig. Well down the base of the lower tier there is a huge boulder set against the wall. Immediately to the right of the boulder there is an obvious and continuous fracture which is the line of the route; initially a chimney, then a corner and finally a long steep crack to the terrace near its right-hand end. Above the terrace an overhang is climbed and the topmost rocks of Great Ridge are reached.

Immediately to the north of the Great Ridge is the prominent dark slash of the *Great Gully*, climbed by W. H. Murray and D. Scott (270 m, Very Difficult). At the top of the gully the right fork was taken. The left fork is the more direct finish, climbed by D. Haworth and Miss J. Tester (45 m, Very Severe). The area of broken rocks to the north of the Great

Gully is *Winter Buttress*, and to its north is *Pinnacle Ridge* which looks impressive from below, but the pinnacles are only steep parts of the ridge, which is just a scramble. The steep east faces of both pinnacles have given hard climbs on rock which is not up to the usual Garbh Bheinn standard.

The next major feature of the mountain is the *North-East Buttress*, a 350 m high buttress formed by four rock tiers separated by grass ledges. The topmost tier appears from below as a steep tower, and below it the most conspicuous feature of the third tier is the Leac Mhor, the huge smooth slab topped by an overhanging band of rock, the Turret. The classic climb on the North-East Buttress is *Route Two* by B. K. Barber and J. Lomas (330 m, Very Difficult). The slabby first tier is ascended directly, and the second tier near its left edge to reach the slanting grass ledge below the Leac Mhor. The ascent of this great slab and the rocks above is the crux of the climb, whether one takes the Direct Route to the left of the Turret (Severe), or the spectacular Turret Variation (Very Difficult). For the latter route one makes a long ascending traverse to the top right-hand corner of Leac Mhor, climbs a short overhang and traverses left onto the front of the Turret, and so to the top. *Route One* on *North-East Buttress* diverges from *Route Two* on the second tier, taking a long rising traverse to the right by an obvious ledge, and then aiming for the top wall to the right of the Leac Mhor (330 m, Difficult), W. H. Murray, J. K. W. Dunn and A. M. MacAlpine. Finally, there is the *North Face*, the slabby buttress which rises above Lochan Coire an Iubhair (150 m, Difficult), B. K. Barber and J. Lomas.

Sgurr Dhomhnuill (888 m)

Sgurr Dhomhnuill is by a few metres the highest mountain in Ardgour. Situated as it is in the centre of the district, it is very remote, yet it is a prominent landmark which is clearly visible from many points. From the east, as one travels up the side of Loch Linnhe, the peak is clearly seen at the head of Glen Scaddle; from the west end of Loch Eil the steep summit cone appears above the hills at the head of Glen Garvan, and the view from Acharacle up Loch Shiel includes a distant view of the peak. It is from Strontian, however, that one gets the closest view of the mountain, 10 km distant at the head of the Strontian River.

There are three principal ridges: the north-east dropping into Glen Scaddle, the south ridge linking with the subsidiary top Sgurr na h-Ighinn and then turning west to drop towards the Strontian Glen,

39

and the north-west ridge over Druim Garbh which extends as a broad featureless shoulder for several kilometres westwards to the Glenhurich Forest.

The best route up Sgurr Dhomhnuill is from Strontian. One can drive up the Strontian Glen as far as the entrance to the Ariundle Nature Reserve, at which point the mountain is 9 km distant. The walk through the magnificent pine and oak woods of the reserve is an excellent start to the day, and gradually the forest road climbs high above the Strontian River to give a fine view of the mountain. In 5 km one reaches the abandoned Feith Dhomhnuill lead mines and crosses the stream to climb easy grassy slopes to the Druim Leac a' Sgiathain, the narrow ridge leading to Sgurr na h-Ighinn. This top can be bypassed if one wishes by a rising traverse along a broad terrace on its north-west face, and the col south of Sgurr Dhomhnuill is reached. The final ascent goes up the south ridge in two steps, with a short level section at mid-height.

An alternative route from Strontian is to drive to the highest point of the road to Loch Doilet and climb along the broad ridge, studded with lochans, to Druim Garbh and so to Sgurr Dhomhnuill by its north-west ridge. This route is certainly shorter and involves less climbing than the one described above, but it is less interesting, lacking in particular the beautiful approach through the Ariundle Forest.

The ascent from the east, by Glen Scaddle, is very long, the round trip from the foot of the glen to Sgurr Dhomhnuill and back being about 30 km. The track up Glen Scaddle gives the impression of going on for ever, and at the point where the glen divides into three one should climb the ridge between Gleann Mhic Phail and Gleann na Cloiche Sgoilte direct to the summit.

Beinn na h-Uamha (762 m), **Sgurr na h-Eanchainne** (730 m)

Two more hills in the south-east corner of Ardgour may be briefly mentioned before proceeding north-west. Beinn na h-Uamha is on the north side of Glen Gour about 7 km up the glen from Sallachan. It is likely to be of interest only to collectors of Corbetts. There is a path up the glen past the ruins of Tigh Ghlinnegabhar, ending 1½ km further and from that point one has to cross the river and climb the south-east ridge of the hill. Sgurr na h-Eanchainne is the steep hill rising directly behind Ardgour village. It is prominent in views up and down the Great Glen, and it in turn commands very fine views. The most direct ascent by the cascading waterfall called MacLean's Towel involves an approach through the policies of Ardgour House, and permission must be sought before this route is taken. A better alternative is to start a couple of kilometres north of the village at the Clan MacLean burial ground and climb the grassy ridge directly above towards the col between Sgurr na h-Eanchainne and Beinn na Cille. Just before reaching this col one can head round to the south and climb to the sharp summit. Two kilometres west, the flat top of Meall Dearg Choire nam Muc is only a few metres lower according to the Ordnance Survey map, and is not as fine a viewpoint as the Sgurr. It can be easily climbed from Sallachan at the foot of Glen Gour.

Carn na Nathrach (786 m), Druim Tarsuinn (770 m)

The central part of Ardgour is a tangle of rugged hills around the upper reaches of Glen Hurich, Glen Scaddle and the Cona Glen. Glen Hurich offers the shortest and easiest approach to these hills for one can drive from Strontian to Kinlochan at the foot of the glen and with permission one might even continue a further 6 km to the bothy at Resourie. This remote cottage just below the tree-line is a good base for exploring the wilds of central Ardgour, and is also a possible stopping place on the south to north crossing of the district. Carn na Nathrach is the highest point of the ridge on the south side of Glen Hurich which extends east to the head of Glen Scaddle. The ascent from Resourie is short; follow the path east for $\frac{1}{2}$ km, cross the river and climb due south on the west side of the prominent deep gully on the north side of Beinn Mheadhoin. Once on the ridge, traverse east to the summit of Carn na Nathrach; at one point the ridge becomes narrow and rocky for a short distance. Druim Tarsuinn is the highest point of the long ridge on the south side of the Cona Glen. The quickest route from Resourie is to climb north beside the stream which comes down from Teanga Chorrach to reach the head of Coire an t-Searraich and the Bealach an Sgriodain, and from there climb $\frac{1}{2}$ km south-east to the peak.

North of the Cona Glen and on the south side of Loch Eil there is a range of smooth rounded hills with some extensive forested areas on their northern slopes. At the eastern end of this range is Stob Coire a' Chearcaill (770 m), whose steep eastern corrie is well seen from Fort William. The other sides of the hill are rather featureless. The shortest ascent is from the south, starting near the foot of the Cona Glen.

41

Sgurr Ghiubhsachain (849 m)

The north-west corner of Ardgour is dominated by a very fine mountain, Sgurr Ghiubhsachain, a steep and rocky peak between Loch Shiel and the head of the Cona Glen. It is well seen from Glenfinnan, and with Beinn Odhar Bheag it makes the superb mountainous setting for Loch Shiel. Its north-west side drops steeply into the loch, and further north-east some of its lower peaks have steep slabby faces overlooking the loch.

A good traverse of the mountain can be made by its east and north ridges, and the best point of departure is the bridge over the Callop River at the foot of the Callop Glen. There is a good path up the glen past Callop cottage, and in 3 km one can leave the path and climb the ridge over Meall na Cuartaige to Sgurr Craoibhe a' Chaorainn (775 m). The descent from this peak south-westwards is quite steep and rocky for a short distance just below the summit, and one should keep to the east, i.e. left if descending, to find an easy descent to the grassy ridge which continues down to the col and then west to Sgurr Ghiubhsachain. The last part of the ascent is again steep, and one has to pick a route upwards by slabs and grassy ledges to finish suddenly at the large cairn. The descent down the north ridge is steep and rocky in places, but with good route-finding there need be no difficulty. Towards the foot of the ridge there is a steep drop over a rocky crag, and it is best to traverse east onto the Coire Ghiubhsachain side of the ridge to avoid it. From Geusachan cottage at the foot of the ridge there is a 5 km walk back to the day's starting point along the Forestry Commission road. (Note that the River Callop cannot be crossed at its outflow into Loch Shiel). The traverse of Sgurr Ghiubhsachain can be made a good deal longer by including the undulating ridge north of Sgurr Craobh a' Chaorainn over Sgorr nan Cearc and Meall a' Bhainne. The north-west side of this ridge has several buttresses overlooking Loch Shiel. K. Schwartz has reported that the best of these buttresses is just west of and below the top of Meall Doire na Mnatha at Map Ref. 895768. Some eight climbs have been done on this crag which is about 300 m long and 100 m high. Its southern end is characterised by two obvious chimneys, the centre is formed by a steep slab wall with easier angled rock on the far north. The crag is best approached from Geusachan cottage.

Beinn Resipol (845 m)

Sunart is a small district sandwiched between Loch Shiel and Loch

Sunart. From the climber's point of view its main feature of interest is Beinn Resipol which stands in solitary splendour in the centre of the district. The mountain is surrounded by rough moorland from which the summit rises in steep and in places rocky slopes. Being an isolated mountain, it commands a very extensive panorama, particularly westwards to the seaboard from Mull north to Skye. It is for its views that Beinn Resipol is renowned, and it is a mountain which should if possible be climbed on a good day.

The traditional route of ascent of Beinn Resipol starts at Strontian, though this is by no means the shortest way. It follows the old miners' track shown on the Ordnance Survey map which climbs north-west from Strontian over the shoulder of Beinn Resipol and drops into Coire an t-Suidhe. From the highest point of this track one should continue down to the first bend and then strike west across a col named Meall an t-Slugain to reach the ridge of the mountain which is followed west to the summit.

The ascent can equally well be made from the shore of Loch Sunart, and the distance is shorter than from Strontian. Possible starting points are Ardery (it is not advisable to attempt to drive up the steep rough road to this deserted farm), Bunalteachan (keep to the Allt Eachain to get above the trees as soon as possible) and Resipole, where there is a good path through the woods on the south side of the Allt Mhic Chiarain.

Another interesting route to Beinn Resipol is from Achnanellan on the south shore of Loch Shiel. There is no path across the Claish Moss from Acharacle, so one should if possible hire a boat to reach Achnanellan, from where there is a path up the mountain.

Walks and Paths

There are several long cross-country walks through Ardgour, most of which involve rough going which is typical of this part of the Western Highlands.

Strontian to Sallachan by Glen Gour. Take the forest road through the Ariundle Nature Reserve, and follow the lower road out of the forest past the ruined cottages at Ceann a' Chreagain. Continue along the trackless upper reaches of the Strontian River and over the narrow pass to Glen Gour where a path is eventually joined on the south side of the river to reach Sallachan (19 km).

Strontian to Callop by Resourie. This is a long walk, full of variety, which takes one through the heart of Ardgour. It may be taken in two stages, staying overnight in Resourie bothy in which case one would have to carry a much heavier rucksack. From Strontian the hill road to Polloch is taken as far as Kinlochan at the head of Loch Doilet, and then the forest road up Glen Hurich is followed to its end near Resourie. The next objective is to cross the Bealach an Sgriodain, 2 km north-east of Resourie; the most direct route is to climb up beside the steep stream which comes down from Teanga Chorrach to the head of its eastern tributary, and then cross the level upper bowl of Coire an t-Searraich to the bealach. Now descend north-east, cross the headwaters of the River Cona and make for the pass on the north side of the glen which leads to the Callop Glen. At this pass a good path is joined, and followed down past Callop cottage to reach the A830 road 2 km east of Glenfinnan (27 km).

Strontian to Conaglen House (*Loch Linnhe*). Follow the route described above to Resourie, and continue up Glen Hurich past Lochan Dubh and walk down the whole length of Glen Scaddle where there is a path for most of the way (32 km).

Conaglen House to Callop. Walk up the Cona Glen which is pleasantly wooded in its lower reaches, but bare beyond the ruin at Corrlarach. There is a rough track to within a couple of kilometres of the pass at the head of the Callop Glen, and the path down this glen leads to the A830 road (20 km). It is also possible to go from the Cona Glen to Loch Eil by Glen Garvan. The best route seems to be by the unnamed col at the head of the North Garvan River.

4

Moidart

Beinn Odhar Mhor (870 m) 851791
Beinn Odhar Bheag (882 m) 846778
Rois-Bheinn (882 m) 756778
An Stac (814 m) 763793
Sgurr na Ba Glaise (874 m) 771776
An t-Slat-bheinn (823 m) 783779
Druim Fiaclach (869 m) 792792
Beinn Mhic Cedidh (783 m) 828788
Croit Bheinn (663 m) 811773
Sgurr Dhomhuill Mor (713 m) 740759

MAP: Ordnance Survey 1:50,000 (2nd Series) Sheet 40.

Moidart is the district lying to the north-west of Loch Shiel; it is bounded on the north by Loch Eilt and on its seaward side by Loch Ailort. It is a land of striking contrast between the low-lying south-western corner which in places is beautifully wooded and cultivated, and the rest of the district which is wild, mountainous and almost totally uninhabited except at a few places round its perimeter. The highest mountains in Moidart are in the north: Rois-Bheinn over-looking Loch Ailort, and Beinn Odhar Mhor and Beinn Odhar Bheag above the head of Loch Shiel. The heart of the district, where the headwaters of the Moidart and Glenaladale rivers rise on the steep sides of Croit Bheinn, is utterly remote.

The road round the northern and western perimeter of Moidart from Glenfinnan to Lochailort (A830), and from there to Acharacle (A861) gives access to most of the district, and practically all the mountains are within easy reach of this road. The West Highland Railway from Fort William to Mallaig goes along the northern edge of Moidart, and there are stations at Glenfinnan and Lochailort. An excursion boat sails the length of Loch Shiel from Acharacle to the head of the loch and back in the summer months from June to August inclusive. Accommodation is available in hotels at Acharacle, Glenuig, Lochailort and Glenfinnan, and also in many houses offering bed and breakfast and in caravans to let.

First impressions of Moidart may well be gained from the road round its perimeter. As one approaches from Fort William along the north shore of Loch Eil the western horizon is dominated by the bulk of Beinn Odhar Mhor and Beinn Odhar Bheag, the two tops being linked by a high ridge. At Glenfinnan there is a National Trust for Scotland Visitor Centre, and the classic view of Loch Shiel stretching into the distance between its enclosing mountains is well seen from the hillside behind the Centre, or from the top of the monument which commemorates the 1745 Jacobite rising. Further west the road crosses a low pass and drops to Loch Eilt. At this point the northern edge of Moidart appears as a series of wild and inhospitable corries. The deserted cottage at Essan on the south side of Loch Eilt offers shelter for walkers and climbers.

The road continues alongside the River Ailort, and the west coast is reached at the head of Loch Ailort where there is a fish farming enterprise. A few kilometres south-west along the loch several small islands almost close its narrow entrance, and the inner loch is over-looked on its south-east side by the steep, craggy and in places wooded slopes of Rois-Bheinn and An Stac. Beyond Roshven Farm the hills become much lower, and the western tip of Moidart, over which the road passes through Glen Uig, is a knobbly moorland dotted with countless lochans. The road returns to sea-level at Loch Moidart and one enters the beautifully wooded south-western corner of Moidart. At the head of the loch one can turn off into Glen Moidart which penetrates for many kilometres into the desolate hinterland of the district, though only the first 3 km are possible for cars.

The main road continues over another low pass and drops down to Shiel Bridge and Acharacle through the only part of Moidart that shows much sign of cultivation. At this point there are very fine views across the west end of Loch Shiel towards Beinn Resipol. At Shiel Bridge a narrow road goes north for 4 km along the right bank of the River Shiel to end at Doirlinn on the sandy shore of Loch Moidart. In the foreground Castle Tioram stands on a rocky knoll which at high tide becomes an island; beyond are the wooded shores of Eilan Shona, the beautiful but very private island which straddles the entrance to Loch Moidart. Although far from the mountains, this corner of Moidart should not be missed; the castle with its surrounding loch and islands, crags and woods, epitomises the romantic image of the West Highland coast.

Moidart is closely associated with Prince Charles Edward Stuart and the ill-fated Jacobite rising of 1745. After the Prince's landing at Loch nan Uamh at the end of July he moved south to stay at Kinlochmoidart House for several days. From there he crossed to Dalelia on Loch Shiel and was rowed up the loch to Glenaladale by MacDonald men. Next day he continued by boat to Glenfinnan at the head of the loch where his standard was unfurled on 19th August.

Beinn Odhar Mhor (870 m), Beinn Odhar Bheag (882 m), Beinn Mhic Cedidh (783 m)

Turning now to the mountains of Moidart, we shall start at Glenfinnan where Beinn Odhar Bheag and Beinn Odhar Mhor overlook the head of Loch Shiel. The south-east side of these mountains drops steeply into the loch in continuous craggy slopes, wooded along the lochside, but the terrain is too rough to be considered a good route of ascent or descent. From Glenfinnan the two summits are not well seen, being hidden beyond the rather characterless lower slopes of Beinn Odhar Mhor; however, it is up this north-east side of the mountain that the ascent is usually made.

The most interesting route is to start in Glenfinnan village, opposite the Stage House Inn, and cross the Amhainn Shlatach. (There is no bridge, but unless the burn is in spate there should be no difficulty in crossing). Now follow the north-west bank of the Allt na h-Aire for over a kilometre and then climb up the hillside westwards into the narrow ravine which leads to Lochan nan Sleubhaich. From this lochan continue south-westwards along the knobbly ridge over Pt. 529 m to the eastern spur of Beinn Odhar Mhor called Sgurr na Boineid, and then turn west up this ridge to the summit. The upper part of this route commands good views of Loch Shiel. In very misty weather it may be better from Lochan nan Sleubhaich to go west through a little col holding two tiny lochans and reach the stream beyond; this stream can be easily followed uphill through a ravine to the upper corrie and so directly to the summit of Beinn Odhar Mhor.

If the Amhainn Shlatach is in spate and impossible to cross at Glenfinnan, it will be necessary to start the ascent about $2\frac{1}{2}$ km to the west. The northern corries of Beinn Odhar Mhor are rather rough, and the walking hard through tussocky grass; the best going is found along the eastern side of the corrie, across the flank of An t-Sleubhaich and up the stream just mentioned.

At the summit of Beinn Odhar Mhor there is a fine view westwards to the Rois-Bheinn group, but Loch Shiel is hidden. The ridge south-wards to Beinn Odhar Bheag is broad at first, but becomes narrower (almost exposed) as one goes round the head of Coire nan Clach and climbs steeply to the pointed summit of the peak on which there is only a small cairn. The view from this peak down to the fiord-like depths of Loch Shiel is very fine. The return to Glenfinnan is best made by retracing one's steps along the outward route unless one is con-templating a longer day by, for example, continuing north-westwards across the Bealach a' Choire Bhuidhe to Beinn Mhic Cedidh, and then descending its narrow north ridge to reach the Glenfinnan-Lochailort road at the east end of Loch Eilt.

The only recorded rock-climbing in Moidart is on a small buttress on the south-east side of Beinn Odhar Mhor on the steep hillside above Loch Shiel. This crag, named Shiel Buttress, is at a height of about 400 m on the spur called Sgurr an Iubhair (Map Ref. 859780), and the approach to it along the shore of Loch Shiel is rough going, so it is probably better to follow the route already described to Beinn Odhar Mhor as far as Lochan nan Sleubhaich (or possibly farther) and then make a descending traverse across the hillside to reach the buttress. The following two routes have been recorded on Shiel Buttress:—

The Rising (125 m, Severe) R. N. Campbell and A. W. Ewing. The front of the buttress is divided by a dark overhung recess high up. Start at the lowest rocks of the left-hand section. Climb to a wide ledge where the buttress steepens (50 m). Climb up rightwards and then back left up a steep shelf to a small stance below overhangs (25 m). Climb by grooves and cracks to the top (50 m). (S.M.C.J., Vol. XXIX, No. 161, p. 298).

Mic (100 m, Very Severe) S. J. Crymble and K. Schwartz. Climb the obvious groove near the left-hand end of the loch-facing wall and go up to a big perched block on a ledge (35 m). Go leftwards to the stance of The Rising below overhangs (17 m). Move right and up to overhang vertically above the perched block. Use sling on a chockstone in the overhang to gain the wall above, which is climbed trending slightly left (48 m). (S.M.C.J., Vol. XXIX, No. 162, p. 408).

Rois-Bheinn (882 m), **Sgurr na Ba Glaise** (874 m),
An t-Slat-bheinn (823 m), **Druim Fiaclach** (869 m), **An Stac** (814 m)

The other important group of mountains in Moidart is Rois-Bheinn and its neighbours near the head of Loch Ailort. Rois-Bheinn in particular is an outstanding mountain, one of the few in the Western

Highlands which rises directly from the western seaboard, and consequently it commands an uninterrupted view of the Sea of the Hebrides. By itself it is a fine, but quite easy climb; taken with its four neighbouring peaks it is one of the best mountain traverses in the Western Highlands.

The topography of the group is as follows:—Rois-Bheinn, the highest peak, rises directly above the narrow entrance of Loch Ailort, and from its twin summit a long ridge extends for several kilometres eastwards and then north-east over the peaks of Sgurr na Ba Glaise, An t-Slat-bheinn and Druim Fiaclach. The northern side of this ridge encloses the big grassy Coire a' Bhuiridh, while the south side (as for as An t-Slat-bheinn) overlooks the head of Glen Moidart. The very prominent conical peak of An Stac stands by itself to the north of the main ridge between Loch Ailort and Coire a' Bhuiridh.

There are two easy routes of ascent of Rois-Bheinn. One is the long broad west ridge which starts near Roshven Farm and leads directly to the top. The other is by the Alisary Burn, following a rather overgrown path on the south side of the burn, and then a tributary south-eastwards into Coire na Cnamha where a dry stone dyke leads right up to the head of the corrie and onto the ridge north-east of Rois-Bheinn. Of the two tops, the eastern one, which is the Trig Point, may be the higher; but the western one, only 4 m lower, is the point with the view, having on a clear day a quite unexcelled panorama of the western seas and islands.

The Alisary Burn is also a convenient approach to An Stac. The final ascent is quite steep, but one can pick a route almost anywhere up the west or north side of the peak with plenty of scrambling on the many rock outcrops if one wishes.

The complete traverse of the four or five peaks of this group is best done (if the day is fine) from north-east to south-west, for going in that direction the seaward views are always in front. The first peak to be climbed is Druim Fiaclach, and the most convenient starting point is Inverailort where there is a rather unsightly collection of buildings, some of them relics of the Second World War. A track from the Glenshian Lodge Hotel leads past these buildings towards the wooded knoll Tom Odhar, and on the south side of the knoll a path leads through a little pass and contours above the Allt a' Bhuiridh for a few hundred metres before disappearing. Continue up the corrie, crossing the main stream, and follow the tributary which has its source in the tiny lochan $\frac{1}{2}$ km north of Druim Fiaclach. The going is very easy up the grassy corrie, but the last hundred metres of climbing is rather steeper and rockier. The name of the mountain—Druim Fiaclach, meaning the toothed ridge—refers to the east-south-east ridge which has some rocky towers on its crest, but is not part of this traverse. The summit of the peak and the south-west ridge leading to its lower top have a precipitous face to the south-east overlooking Coire Reidh, the highest recess of Glen Aladale, and the walk along this ridge is delightful. The same can be said for its continuation along the undulating crest of An t-Slat-bheinn, only now the long steep slopes on one's left plunge down into the head of Glen Moidart, and in front the north face of Sgurr na Ba Glaise looms up. This peak is in some respects the finest of the group, having a very precipitous north face cleft by a long gully. The descent north-west to the Bealach an Fhiona is easy, as is the final climb to Rois-Bheinn, the culminating point of the traverse.

An Stac can be included at the end of the day by returning almost to the Bealach an Fhiona and then descending north to a lower col from which An Stac is climbed by its south ridge. From its summit the return to the day's starting point can be made northwards and then north-east over Seann Chruach to reach the path on the south side of Tom Odhar.

The preceding traverse can be made much more interesting, and also rather longer, by starting at the east end of Loch Eilt and climbing Beinn Mhic Cedidh by its fine north ridge. Then a long descent and traverse westwards brings one to the foot of the east-south-east ridge of Druim Fiaclach, and this ridge is climbed over the little teeth to the top where the 'normal' traverse is joined.

Croit Bheinn (663 m), Sgurr Dhomhuill Mor (713 m)

To mention briefly some of the other hills in Moidart, Croit Bheinn stands at the head of Glen Moidart and is so remote as to be rarely climbed. It is a fine little hill, steep on three sides, particularly the north-west side which is quite rocky.

The high ground to the south of Rois-Bheinn which culminates in Sgurr Dhomhuill Mor is not of particular interest. This peak can be climbed either from Glen Moidart or from Roshven Farm. On the east side of these hills there are some fine corries above Glen Moidart, but the west side is featureless and uninteresting.

Walks and Paths

The best cross-country walk in this district, which shows its pastoral as well as its mountainous aspects, is from the head of Loch Moidart to

Lochailort by Glen Moidart. Four kilometres beyond Glenmoidart House, at the ruins of Assary, one climbs north out of the glen by the steep grassy slopes leading to the Bealach an Fhiona. This is the line of an old cross-country route as is indicated by occasional cairns and the traces of a path near the bealach. On the north side of the pass one descends steeply into Coire a' Bhuiridh, and 3 km down this glen reaches the path to Lochailort through the Tom Odhar gap (16 km from the head of Loch Moidart to Lochailort).

A very pleasant low-level walk can be made, starting at Shiel Bridge and walking down the river to Doirlinn and Castle Tioram, and continuing north then east along the path through the trees on the steep side of Loch Moidart as far as Port a' Bhata. The return to Shiel Bridge can be varied by taking the path below the west face of Beinn Bhreac and past Loch Blain (10 km).

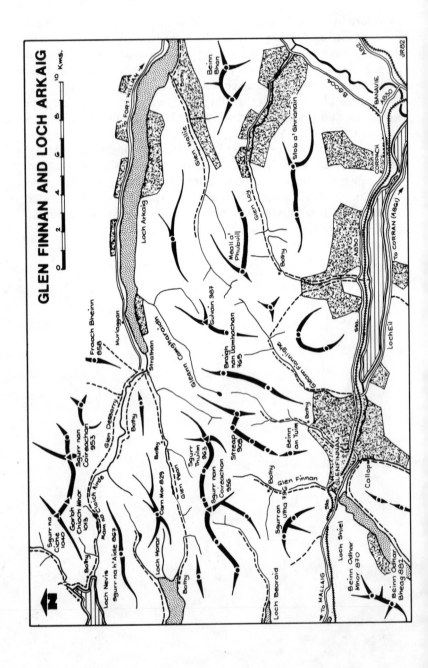

GLEN FINNAN AND LOCH ARKAIG

12. *Sgurr Dhomhnuill from the Strontian Glen.*

13. *Beinn Resipol from Acharacle.*

14. *Castle Tioram, Loch Moidart.*

15. *In Glen Moidart, looking towards Sgurr na Ba Glaise.*

16. On the first pitch of Faradh Dubh, Beinn na Seilg, Ardnamurchan.

17. On the summit crags of Meall nan Con, Ardnamurchan.

18. *Looking west from Druim Fiaclach to Sgurr na Ba Glaise (left), Rois-Bheinn and An Stac (right). On the horizon is the island of Muck.*

19. *An Stac and Rois-Bheinn from Loch Ailort.*

21. *Looking south from the Streap ridge to Loch Sheil, with Beinn Resipol beyond. Beinn Odhar Bheag and Beinn Odhar Mhor are to the right.*

20. *Looking west from Beinn Odhar Mhor to Rois-Bheinn.*

22.   Looking west from the sands of Arisaig to Rum.

23.   At Arieniskill on the Road to the Isles, looking south to Sgurr na Ba Glaise and An Stac.

5

Locheil, Glen Finnan and Morar

Beinn Bhan (796 m) 141858
Gulvain (987 m) 003876
Streap (909 m) 946864
Sgurr Thuilm (963 m) 939879
Sgurr nan Coireachan (956 m) 903880
Sgurr an Utha (796 m) 885839
Carn Mor (829 m) 903910
Sgurr na h-Aide (867 m) 889931
An Stac (718 m) 866889
Sgurr an Eilein Ghiubhais (522 m) 727973

Munro's Tables, Section 10

MAPS: Ordnance Survey 1:50,000 Sheets 40 and 41.

The well defined valley which stretches westwards from the head of Loch Linnhe to the sea at Loch Ailort is one of the most obvious dividing lines in the Western Highlands, and also one of the most important lines of communication for it carries the main road (A830) and the railway from Fort William to Mallaig. It also marks the beginning, as one goes from south to north, of the 'high' mountains, the Munros, and Munro-baggers may be forgiven for thinking that the Western Highlands only start north of the Road to the Isles. About 12 km to the north another east-west valley is formed by Loch Arkaig, Glen Dessarry and Loch Nevis, and between these two valleys are the western part of Lochaber, Morar and Arisaig which together form the subject of this chapter.

This area can itself be divided into three regions of quite different characteristics. To the east, between Loch Eil and Loch Arkaig, there is a region of rather low rounded hills with smooth forested slopes and few features of mountaineering interest. Several long glens—Glen

Mallie, Glen Loy and Gleann Suileag—penetrate into this region, and Beinn Bhan in its north-east corner overlooking the Great Glen is the highest hill. Further west, beyond Gleann Fionnlighe, the mountains become much higher and steeper, and the head of Glen Finnan is surrounded by high ridges and craggy peaks. Further west again, beyond Loch Beoraid, the terrain though no less rugged becomes less mountainous. This district, North and South Morar (with Loch Morar dividing it), is remarkably wild and seldom visited; it is a tangle of rocky hillocks of 500 or 600 m rising above rough undulating moorland. In the more populated parts of the country these hills would be thoroughly explored by rock-climbers, for there are innumerable crags, large and small; here however, in this remote corner of the Highlands they pass almost unnoticed and unknown. Finally, in the south-western corner of the area described in this chapter, is Arisaig, a charming little peninsula of beautiful woodland, rocky headlands and sandy bays. The silver sands which extend northwards from Arisaig village to the River Morar are renowned and justifiably popular in summer, when this corner of the Western Highlands takes on the appearance of a holiday resort.

All the hills in the area described in this chapter, with the exception of a few of the really remote ones in Morar, can be reached within a few hours from the roads along its perimeter. From the climbers' point of view it is the Glen Finnan hills which are likely to hold most interest, and these are all accessible from Glenfinnan village (where there are hotels) or from points on the main road nearby. Alternatively, these hills and those between Glen Pean and Glen Dessarry can be approached from the end of the public road just beyond the west end of Loch Arkaig. There is no accommodation there except in bothies such as A'Chuil (Glen Dessarry), Pean (Glen Pean) and further west at Oban (east end of Loch Morar).

The area described in this chapter is, like Moidart, closely associated with Prince Charles Edward Stuart and the Jacobite rising of 1745. It was at Loch nan Uamh on the Arisaig coast that he landed on 25th July that year, and he finally departed from there on 19th September 1746. The early days of his campaign saw him march along the north side of Loch Eil with his men after the raising of his standard at Glenfinnan. The following year after the Battle of Culloden his flight from Hanoverian troops took him through Morar and over the hills between Glen Finnan and Loch Arkaig three times as he eluded his pursuers. Not surprisingly there are several 'Prince Charlie's Caves' in the area, some of which (for example, the one near Druimindarroch on the shore of Loch nan Uamh) are authentic. Those who nowadays walk and climb among the rugged hills of Morar and Glen Finnan can only admire the fortitude of the Prince and the loyalty of his followers during their weeks of travel and hiding in this wild country.

Beinn Bhan (796 m), **Stob a' Ghrianain** (744 m), **Meall a' Phubuill** (774 m)

The area between Loch Eil and Loch Arkaig has few features of interest until one reaches Gulvain, the first of the Munros. It is an area of rounded hills with smooth contours, and there is much forestry along the lower slopes of the hills above Loch Eil and in Gleann Suileag, Glen Loy and Glen Mallie. Although the hills are not particularly interesting themselves, some of them are very fine viewpoints standing, as they do, just across the Great Glen from Ben Nevis and its high neighbours. This is particularly true of Beinn Bhan which rises between Glen Loy and Glen Mallie a few kilometres west of the Great Glen; on a clear day it commands a superb view of the Lochaber mountains south of Glen Spean. The quickest ascent is from Inverskilavulin in Glen Loy, climbing up the east side of Coire Mhuillin to the highest point which is at the east end of the crescent shaped summit ridge. Coire Bhotrais, the north-western corrie, looks fine but does not appear to hold out any climbing possibilities.

Another pleasant short ascent from Glen Loy is Stob a' Ghrianain. This top is the highest point of the long level hill Druim Fada which rises above the east end of Loch Eil, and it too is a fine viewpoint. The ascent can easily be made from the cottage at Puiteachan in Glen Loy where there is a fine stand of old Scots pines at the west end of the Glen Loy Forest. There is a good half-day walk through Gleann Suileag and Glen Loy from Fassfern on Locheilside to Glen Loy Lodge. It calls for little detailed description; about $4\frac{1}{2}$ km up the good track in Gleann Suileag one comes to the Glensulaig bothy. The path is not well defined for the next 2 km, but it continues well up on the north side of the glen and leads to Achnanellan in Glen Loy. Finally one walks down the narrow and almost invariably traffic-free road to the foot of this glen ($17\frac{1}{2}$ km). There is a path up the hillside north of Glensulaig bothy which gives an easy route to Meall a' Phubuill.

Another longer walk between Loch Eil and Loch Arkaig links Gleann Fionnlighe and Glen Mallie. Starting at the head of Loch Eil, one takes the rough road up Fionnlighe to the cottage at Wauchan, and continues

3 km further to the footbridge over the Allt a' Choire Reidh. Thereafter the going over the watershed on the south-east side of Gulvain is trackless for several kilometres. In due course a rough shelter in Glen Mallie is reached, and a good track leads down the glen past the ruined cottage of Glenmallie to Inver Mallie, where the bothy provides good shelter. The last few kilometres of this walk down Glen Mallie and along the side of Loch Arkaig are particularly attractive, (26 km from the A830 road to the east end of Loch Arkaig).

Gulvain (987 m)

The mountainous central part of the area described in this chapter starts with Gulvain (alternative form Gaor Bheinn, also spelt Culvain). This is a massive mountain consisting of an isolated ridge running roughly south to north on the west side of the watershed between Gleann Fionnlighe and Glen Mallie. Its two tops are connected by a high ridge which dips only slightly between them. The ascent is most usually made from the south, by Gleann Fionnlighe. Follow the route just described from the head of Loch Eil to the footbridge over the Allt a' Choire Reidh. Beyond this bridge the path continues up the lower hillside of Gulvain for a short distance before fading out, however there is no need for a path as the south shoulder up which one climbs is an easy but unrelenting grass slope leading over a minor top to the south summit, which is the trig point (961 m). The ridge continues north-east, broad at first, but beyond the col it becomes quite narrow and one is very much aware of the long steep drops on both sides. The higher, north-east summit (987 m) has a large cairn. The rocks of Gulvain are largely a banded granite or 'granite-gneiss', and on the west side of the mountain this forms steep slabs which are no use for climbing, and are best avoided. So steep is this side of Gulvain that stags shot there are reputed to fall right down the mountainside.

It is also quite possible to climb Gulvain from the north. Three possibilities suggest themselves: First, from Kinlocharkaig one can cross the steep-sided ridge of Leac na Carnaich to reach Gleann Camgharaidh from which the very steep ascent of the north-west face of Gulvain has to be made, unless one keeps well to the north to reach the ridge lower down. Secondly, if one has a canoe in which to cross Loch Arkaig, a very fine approach to Gulvain can be made up Gleann Camgharaidh; there is a beautiful remnant of ancient pine forest at the foot of this glen. The third possibility is to approach Gulvain from the east end of Loch Arkaig by Glen Mallie; this is a long walk and a bicycle would be useful.

Braigh nan Uamhachan (765 m)

There is another good hill-walk to be done from Gleann Fionnlighe, namely Braigh nan Uamhachan, the highest point of the ridge on the west side of the glen. The best way is to strike up the hillside northwards from Wauchan and follow the ridge over several tops to the highest point. This is a very interesting traverse which would undoubtedly be better known if the Braigh had the extra height to bring it to Munro status.

Streap (909 m), Streap Comhlaidh (898 m), Beinn an Tuim (810 m)

Going westwards, the next peak of interest is Streap, which is the highest point of the very fine ridge between Gleann Dubh Lighe and Glen Finnan. The southernmost hill of this ridge is Beinn an Tuim, situated 4 km north-east of Glenfinnan. North-eastwards along the ridge the peaks are Meall an Uillt Chaoil (844 m), Stob Coire nan Cearc (887 m), Streap and finally turning a short distance south-east Streap Comhlaidh. Beyond this summit the main ridge continues north-east, gradually dropping towards the head of Loch Arkaig.

Streap is not only the highest, but also the finest peak of this group, and it is possibly the finest peak in the area described in this chapter. Seen from the north-east it looks very fine, with the steep north ridge surmounted by its pointed summit. It also has a very narrow, almost exposed south-west ridge, fine corries to the north-east and south, and the north-west face drops with remarkable steepness to the pass at the head of Glen Finnan. The south corrie, Coire Chuirn, contains the remains of an immense landslip which has detached from the headwall along a fault line, and some of the rocks high up in the corrie are still unstable as signs of recent rockfall show. One should be very careful if scrambling up or down the corrie. The line of the fault crosses the south-west ridge and forms an easy-angled rake on the Glen Finnan side sloping down the steep hillside towards Corryhully.

From the south there are two possible lines of approach to the Streap ridge: Gleann Dubh Lighe and Glen Finnan. The former is, in the author's opinion, the more attractive glen, and the track along the west side of Dubh Lighe burn goes through some beautiful stretches of mixed woodland and forestry plantations, with the stream tumbling nearby over many little falls and through dark pools. From the point where the track ends at the upper limit of the trees one can climb north-west to reach Beinn an Tuim, and thereafter continue with quite a lot of up and downhill work along the ridge to Streap. Just before reaching this top the ridge becomes very narrow and exposed for a short distance, its crest little more than a sharp edge of rock. Turning south-east, another narrow ridge leads to Streap Comhlaidh. From there the descent can be made southwards, along a grassy ridge which, beyond a minor top, plunges down to Gleann Dubh Lighe where another good path on the east side of the stream is found. This leads to the bothy, Upper Drimsallie, near the tree line and (if one stays on the east side of the stream) down a rather overgrown path through the forest past Drimsallie Mill to the main road.

Streap can also be climbed from Strathan at the head of Loch Arkaig. Cross the River Pean, climb south onto the ridge near Leac na Carnaich and follow this ridge for $3\frac{1}{2}$ km over many knolls to Streap Comhlaidh and Streap. The ascent from the head of Gleann a' Chaorainn is probably best avoided unless one is prepared for some very steep climbing.

Glen Finnan is less attractive than Dubh Lighe, lacking any features to soften the bare hillsides of its lower reaches. The Forestry Commission have done a lot of planting in this part of the glen, and its appearance will in due course be greatly altered. The two features for which the glen is best known are both at its foot, and both are man-made. The Glenfinnan Monument stands on the grassy sward at the head of Loch Shiel, and commemorates the 1745 rising. The figure at its top is a bearded highland soldier, and not the Prince as is commonly supposed. One kilometre away to the north the viaduct of the West Highland Railway strides across the entrance to Glen Finnan in 20 great arches; it is one of the most dramatic railway bridges in the country. The National Trust for Scotland have a Visitor Centre and car park at the roadside opposite the Monument.

Three and a half kilometres up Glen Finnan stands the new Corryhully Lodge, whose suburban appearance is rather out of character with its surroundings. Below the lodge by the riverside is Corryhully bothy, which is available as an unlocked, but very primitive shelter. A short distance beyond Corryhully the glen splits, one part forming the Coire

Thollaidh which is surrounded by high peaks, and the other part being the narrow, steep-sided pass which leads to Loch Arkaig.

The ascent of Streap from Glen Finnan is most easily made by crossing the river by the footbridge a short distance upstream from Corryhully and climbing diagonally up the steep hillside in an easterly direction to reach the easy-angled rake already mentioned. This rake leads to the south-west ridge not far from the summit.

Sgurr Thuilm (963 m), Sgurr nan Coireachan (956 m)

Coire Thollaidh is enclosed by a high ridge forming a great horseshoe of peaks. On the east is Sgurr Thuilm, on the west is Sgurr nan Coireachan, and between them are the lower peaks of Beinn Gharbh (825 m) and Meall an Tarmachain (826 m). The traverse of this ridge is another fine expedition, which gives quite a long day when one adds to the mountains the walk up and down Glen Finnan. Five kilometres up the glen the path crosses the main stream descending from Coire Thollaidh (no bridge, possibly difficult to cross in spate) and straight ahead the grassy raidge of Druim Coire a' Bheithe gives a very straightforward climb over a minor top to Sgurr Thuilm. The ridge westwards over the two intermediate summits is very pleasant, and there are fine glimpses down the steep and craggy north side of the ridge into the narrow depths of Glen Pean, however it is only when one reaches Sgurr nan Coireachan that the view over the wilds of Morar opens out. On the descent down the south-east ridge one has to cross the little top of Sgurr a' Choire Riabhaich (852 m); the ridge at this point is steep on both flanks, and some care is needed when descending in thick weather. (In bad conditions it might be better to ascend by this ridge and do the traverse in a clockwise direction). Coire Carnaig to the south-west is a grand rocky corrie, showing a fine expanse of glaciated slabs, and near the foot of the Allt a' Choire Charnaig there is a tiny reservoir providing water for the hydro-electric generator which supplies Corryhully Lodge.

The north side of the Sgurr Thuilm—Sgurr nan Coireachan ridge forms some wild corries overlooking Glen Pean, and the ascent from this glen is a steep, rough scramble. The Pean bothy is a good base, but if the River Pean is in spate it will be impossible to cross at the bothy, and the crossing should be made by the footbridge at the foot of Gleann a' Chaorainn, from where the north-east ridge of Sgurr Thuilm is the obvious route of ascent.

Sgurr an Utha (796 m)

Three kilometres north-west of Glenfinnan are the two peaks of
Fraoch-bheinn (790 m) and Sgurr an Utha. They can both be climbed
in a short half day by the ridge north of the village (Tom na h-Aire). The
reward on a good day is a fine view westwards from the higher top
towards lonely Loch Beoraid and the wilds of Morar, and north-
eastwards towards Streap and Sgurr Thuilm.

Continuing westwards one comes to Morar, a wild land of rocky
hills, undulating moorland and innumerable lochans dotted high up on
the moors. It is a land neglected by climbers and walkers, for the hills
are not high enough to command attention, and the moorland is if
anything too rough to be attractive for cross-country walking. One
walk can, however, be recommended as a way of exploring the wilds of
South Morar. Start at the roadside 2 km west of Glenfinnan at the
bridge over the Allt Feith a' Chatha (cross marked on the map at this
point). Forestry plantings and a rough road up the hillside on the north
make this point unmistakable. Follow the path north-westwards as far
as possible, cross the col and descend to the head of Loch Beoraid. The
house at Kinlochbeoraid is private and locked, but shelter may be
possible in an outhouse. Now follow the path westwards along the
north side of Loch Beoraid to the little hydro-electric power house at
its outflow. From there a path climbs steeply southwards through
beautiful birch glades; near the top, below a great overhanging crag,
another of Prince Charlie's caves can be found under some huge fallen
boulders. Finally the path crosses a very boggy pass and descends to
Arieniskill, 2 km from Lochailort Station. (Needless to say, this walk
should not be done on a Sunday if one is relying on the train for the
return to Glenfinnan).

Carn Mor (829 m), Sgurr na h-Aide (867 m)

North Morar is the long peninsula between Loch Morar and Loch
Nevis. At its landward end between Glen Pean and Glen Dessarry it is
very mountainous and rugged, having something of the character of the
Rough Bounds of Knoydart immediately to the north, and there are
two fine hills, Carn Mor and Sgurr na h-Aide in this area. Both can be
most conveniently climbed from Strathan at the west end of Loch
Arkaig, and A'Chuil bothy is a particularly convenient base. There is a
forestry road up Glen Dessarry from Strathan on the south side of the

river which goes past A'Chuil and ends 2 km further up the glen.There is also a forestry road from Strathan up Glen Pean on the north side of the River Pean.

The ascent of Carn Mor from the east is very straightforward, the ridge from Strathan to the summit being 8 km long and possibly rather monotonous. A shorter route is that from A'Chuil south-westwards up Coire an Eich or one of its bounding ridges. By contrast with the grassy eastern end of the hill, the western end is quite rocky and falls steeply into the glens to the north and south. Two words of warning may be given about this hill; first, in the area between A'Chuil and Pean bothy the magnetic compass has been found to be inaccurate, but this is only likely to be a problem if it is held close to rocks. Second, the steep southern slopes of the hill (particularly above Loch Leum an t-Sagairt) are cut by landslip fissures, some of which are narrow and deep; so care is required, especially if there is snow on the ground.

Sgurr na h-Aide is a very fine hill. It is the prominent pointed peak which one sees from afar off as one approaches along the side of Loch Arkaig. To reach the foot of the east ridge, which is the best route of ascent, one should follow the path on the north side of Glen Dessarry for a kilometre or so beyond the Allt Coire nan Uth. In this way one avoids the newly planted forest in the glen with its numerous obstacles such as young trees and drainage ditches. Then climb westwards onto the end of the ridge, Meall na Sroine, and continue over many knolls and past two delightful little lochans to the final steep peak, where a bit of scrambling may be needed if one climbs directly up to the top. The lower west peak (859 m) is less than a kilometre away along a pleasant ridge. Both the north and south sides of the mountain are very steep. On the north side boiler-plate slabs drop from the summit ridge towards Finiskaig and the Mam na Cloich' Airde; the ascent of this face of the mountain from the head of Loch Nevis is a fine steep scramble, but the descent by the same route requires care. On the south side of the summit the drop to Gleann an Lochain Eanaiche is even steeper, 700 m at an average angle of about 45°; a most impressive mountainside, whether looked at from above or below.

To the west of Sgurr na h-Aide the spine of the North Morar peninsula continues over a series of progressively lower peaks to the isthmus at Tarbet. Beyond, and in the far north-west corner of the peninsula there are three small and very rocky hills which can best be reached from Mallaig. They are well worth a visit by anyone with a day (or even a few hours) to spare while waiting for the ferry to Skye, for they command superb views to the Western Isles and in the opposite direction, up Loch Nevis to the great peak of Sgurr na Ciche. Sgurr an Eilein Ghiubhais (522 m) rises very steeply from Loch Nevis in a series of buttresses and crags, and it is an impressive sight when sailing up the loch. If one could make a landing at the foot of the hill, there would undoubtedly be some very interesting climbing to reach the summit. Carn a' Ghobhair (548 m) and Sgurr Bhuidhe (436 m) face each other across Loch Eireagoraidh, which is accessible from Mallaig by a 4 km path. There is a steep cliff about 60 m high on the south face of Sgurr Bhuidhe, most easily accessible from Bracorina on the north shore of Loch Morar, which is rumoured to give some good climbing.

Walks and Paths

In addition to those walks already mentioned, there are several other fine cross-country routes through the area described in this chapter. The route from Glenfinnan northwards to Strathan at the west end of Loch Arkaig, and from there westwards through Glen Dessarry to the head of Loch Nevis is one of the walkers' trade routes in the Western Highlands, and two other superb passes lead from Strathan to Loch Morar. Brief details of some of these cross-country routes are as follows:—

Fassfern to Strathan. This is the line of a very old route, part of it marked on the 1875 edition of the Ordnance Survey map, but seldom used nowadays so that the paths which once existed have now largely disappeared. From Fassfern take the right-of-way up Gleann Suileag and cross the river at the first possible point after leaving the forest; then cross the pass between Meall Onfhaidh and Aodann Chleireig to descend steeply into Gleann Fionnlighe. Continue north up the east side of the Allt a' Choire Reidh, over the pass at its head into Gleann Camgharaidh, and still keeping due north over the ridge below Leac na Carnaich descend north-west to the bridge over the River Pean near Strathan (15 km).

Glenfinnan to Strathan. This route is very obvious, up the road in Glen Finnan to Corryhully bothy and 2 km further to the crossing of the Allt Coire a' Bheithe. (There is no footbridge at this point, and the crossing may be dangerous if the burn is in spate. There are footbridges about a kilometre up the burn). A path continues north-eastwards towards the pass (471 m) which is a deep gash between Streap and Sgurr Thuilm, and beyond it the descent to Glen Pean should be made on the east side of the Allt a' Chaorainn (14 km).

Gleann Dubh Lighe to Strathan. This is an alternative to the more usual Glen Finnan route. The track to Upper Drimsallie bothy ends 2 km further up the glen. Thereafter the way is indicated intermittently by posts: up to the head of the glen, across the watershed and a kilometre past Lochan a' Chomhlain before climbing 100 m to reach the lowest point of the ridge south-west of Leac na Carnaich. Finally, one descends to the footbridge over the River Pean near Strathan (14 km from the A830 to Strathan).

Strathan to Loch Morar. There are two ways, one through Glen Pean, and the other rather less directly up Glen Dessarry for 6 km and then by Gleann an Lochain Eanaiche. Both these routes are superb, leading through narrow crag-girt glens, past dark lochans and through rocky gorges to the lonely head of Loch Morar. It would be virtually impossible to lose the way on either of these walks, for to stray from the right way would be to find oneself climbing up very steep hillsides. However, the map is inaccurate in showing that the path through Glen Pean goes on the north side of Lochan Leum an t-Sagairt; it is on the south side. There is a path on the south side of the river all the way from Pean bothy to the head of the glen. Having reached the east end of Loch Morar, hardy walkers can continue along the north shore of the loch to Tarbet and Bracorina. An alternative, which gives a fairly strenuous walk for a single day, is to do the circuit from Strathan to the head of Loch Morar and back to Strathan, going by one glen and returning by the other (27 km). An even better expedition would be to take two days for this circuit, spend the night at the head of Loch Morar (possibly in the bothy at Oban), and climb the pointed peak of An Stac (718 m) which rises directly above the head of the loch. In this way one could enter fully into the spirit of isolation and solitude that pervades these lonely mountains.

Glenfinnan to Loch Morar. It is tempting to try to find a route across the very rough and complex terrain between Glen Finnan and Loch Beoraid, but there are no obvious ways, and this particular challenge is left to the reader.

Strathan to Loch Nevis. This right-of-way is the trade route to the west from the head of Loch Arkaig. In Glen Dessarry there is a choice of routes, but unless one wants to call at A'Chuil bothy (in which case the

63

forestry road on the south side of the glen may be preferred) the track by Glendessarry Lodge and Upper Glendessarry is better. Continuing westwards, the path is fairly good as far as the bealach, but the next couple of kilometres past Lochan a' Mhaim are rather rough going. The pass itself, the Mam na Cloich' Airde, is a wild and beautiful place, enclosed by steep craggy hills and the debris of rock falls. The path improves as it drops towards Loch Nevis, showing in places signs of having once been very well constructed. The crossing of the Allt Coire na Ciche is notoriously dangerous when the burn is in spate. Finally one reaches the grassy pastures at the head of the loch and the welcome haven of Sourlies bothy (14 km). It has been suggested by A. E. Robertson that this track may date from the days of herring fishing in Loch Nevis, the track being used for carrying the fish to the markets in the south. This would explain the very good construction of the track at certain points, for example the hairpins above Loch Nevis.

6

Loch Arkaig to Glen Garry

Meall na Teanga (917 m) 220924
Meall Coire Lochain (900 m) 215920
Meall Dubh (837 m) 229932
Sron a' Choire Ghairbh (935 m) 223945
Ben Tee (901 m) 241972
Geal Charn (804 m) 156943
Meall na h-Eilde (838 m) 185946
Sgurr Mhurlagain (879 m) 012944
Fraoch Bheinn (858 m) 986940
Gairich (919 m) 025996
Sgurr an Fhuarain (901 m) 987980
Sgurr Mor (1003 m) 965980
Sgurr Beag (890 m) 959971
An Eag (873 m) 943959
Sgurr nan Coireachan (953 m) 933958
Garbh Chioch Mhor (1013 m) 909961
Sgurr na Ciche (1040 m) 902966
Ben Aden (887 m) 899986

Munro's Tables, Section 10

MAPS: Ordnance Survey 1:50,000 (2nd Series) Sheets 33 and 34.

This slice of the Western Highlands is just as well defined as its neighbours to the south and north. Its southern boundary is Loch Arkaig and Glen Dessarry and its northern boundary is Glen Garry, Loch Quoich and the pass at the west end of the loch which leads to the head of Loch Nevis. On the east the area is bounded by Loch Lochy, one of the long narrow lochs of the Great Glen.

The mountains in the eastern end of this area rise very abruptly from Loch Lochy, their lower slopes being densely forested along the lochside. These mountains, Meall na Teanga, Sron a' Choire Ghairbh and Ben Tee are sometimes called the Clunes hills after the Forestry Commission village of that name at their southern end; however, it is probably more logical to refer to them as the Loch Lochy hills. Going westwards, the hills become progressively lower and there is an extensive tract of country between Loch Arkaig on the south and Glen Garry and Glen Kingie on the north which is rather featureless and of no great interest to the climber. It is an area of rounded hills and some very boggy country. Continuing further west the country is more mountainous, and it is in the western part of the area described in this chapter that we find its highest and grandest mountains. There, round the desolate upper reaches of Glen Kingie, westwards to Glen Dessarry and finally to the head of Loch Nevis, we find a wild and rugged group of mountains which culminate in Sgurr na Ciche, one of the great landmarks of the Western Highlands.

Apart from these high mountains which, in character at least, are part of the Rough Bounds of Knoydart, the other remarkable feature of this area is Glen Kingie. Seventeen kilometres long, it is utterly bleak and devoid of human habitation with the possible exception of the bothy beside the ruined lodge at Kinbreack. The river flows sluggishly in long curves through the boggy grassland of the glen, and only near its lower reaches are there any signs of human activity, and they needless to say are the plantings of the Forestry Commission. Glen Kingie, more than any other glen of the Western Highlands, epitomises the desolate wilderness that is so much a part of this land.

Approach to the hills described in this chapter can be made in several ways. From the south-east the narrow B8005 road from Gairlochy goes to Clunes and then turns west through the dark wooded pass, the Mile Dorcha, and past the waterfall at the foot of Gleann Cia-aig to reach the east end of Loch Arkaig. The road continues, now very narrow with many twists and switchbacks, to the west end of the loch where the public road ends and an unsurfaced private road continues to Strathan where the Pean and Dessarry take their separate ways. Loch Arkaig is a fine loch, wooded along much of its northern side, with some good camping sites. (Permission should be sought at Bunarkaig or from the West Highland Estate Offices in Fort William, who may also be able to give information about caravans and cottages to let). The views westward along the loch include a sharp pointed peak in the distance which turns out to be Sgurr na h-Aide, looking very much like a small version of Sgurr na Ciche.

On the north side of this area access is by the A87 road from Invergarry along Loch Garry, and its continuation westwards past Tomdoun and along the north side of Loch Quoich to end eventually at Kinloch Hourn. This is not such a useful route of access to the mountains described in this chapter as the enlarged Loch Quoich forms a very effective barrier between road and mountains. The Loch Lochy hills can be reached from either Clunes or Kilfinnan near Laggan Locks, and there is a Forestry Commission road along the side of Loch Lochy between these two points.

From the west access to the mountains at the head of Loch Nevis may be possible by boat from Mallaig. The present edition of the Ordnance Survey map is rather misleading in this respect as there is not (as indicated) a regular ferry service to the head of the loch. The present situation is that the operator who runs the mail service between Mallaig and Inverie may sometimes continue up Loch Nevis on a sight-seeing trip, but anyone wishing to land at the head of the loch would have to make special arrangements (Bruce Watt Cruises, Mallaig; Telephone 0687 2233). The post office at Tarbet on the south side of Loch Nevis has recently been closed, and it may be in the future that the boat will only rarely go up the loch beyond Inverie; however, the journey up Loch Nevis by boat is a wonderful experience whether or not one is able to go ashore at the head of the loch.

Accommodation in the area of this chapter is not very plentiful. If one's preference is for hotels, then Spean Bridge, Fort William and Banavie on the south-east side, and Invergarry and Tomdoun on the north side are possible places to stay, but they are all some distance from the hills. If one's preference is for the more spartan shelter of bothies, then Pean (Glen Pean), A'Chuil (Glen Dessarry), Kinbreack (Glen Kingie) and Sourlies (Loch Nevis) are all available. As already mentioned there is good camping on the north side of Loch Arkaig (with permission), and also at Clunes and off the roadside on the north shore of Loch Garry. There are chalets to let at Laggan.

Like the area to the south, the district has many historical associations with the 1745 Jacobite Rising and its aftermath. On the day after the Battle of Culloden Prince Charles fled down the west side of Loch Lochy and westwards through the Mile Dorcha (the dark mile), along Loch Arkaig and into Glen Pean on his way to the coast. Two months later he was back on the mainland after his sojourn in the Hebrides, this time crossing the mountains northwards from Glen Dessarry to Loch Quoich. Later, in August that year, the Prince spent two weeks hiding 'in sundry fast places' near the east end of Loch Arkaig. One of these was a big tree, another a cave in Gleann Cia-aig above the Mile Dorcha. Finally, in September he passed again through the Mile Dorcha and along Loch Arkaig on his last flight to the west coast to board a ship for France. There is also a legend that a considerable amount of

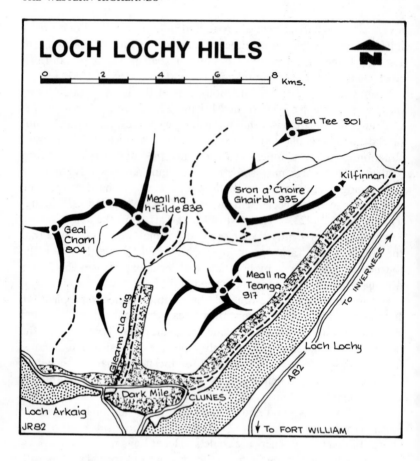

Jacobite treasure and gold was buried either in or close to Loch Arkaig at the time of the 1745 Rising, but there is no record of its subsequent fate. Some optimists have thought that it may still be buried where it was hidden more than two hundred years ago.

The Loch Lochy hills rise very boldly on the west side of that loch, presenting a continuously steep and in some places precipitous hillside with dark forests clinging to the lower slopes along the lochside. The summits themselves are rather rounded and not nearly as rugged as those further west, but they hold some fine corries and Ben Tee, the northern outlier of this group, is a pointed hill that is one of the most prominent landmarks in the Great Glen. To the west and north-west

68

24. *In the Callop Glen, looking north to Beinn an Tuim and Streap.*

25. *Looking down Loch Shiel from Glenfinnan, Sgurr Ghiubhsachain on the left.*

26. *Looking east along Loch Beoraid from the crag above Prince Charlie's Cave. The Glen Finnan hills are in the distance.*

27. *At Corryhully bothy in Glen Finnan, looking north to Sgurr Thuilm.*

28. *Kinbreack bothy in Glen Kingie, looking towards Gairich.*

29. *Glen Dessarry, with Carn Mor (left) and Sgurr na h-Aide (right).*

30. Ben Nevis and the Lochaber mountains from Bunarkaig on Loch Lochy.

31. *Looking towards Sgurr Thuilm and Sgurr nan Coireachan at the head of Loch Arkaig.*

32.   Streap and Sgurr Thuilm from Strathan at the head of Loch Arkaig.

33.   *Sgurr na h-Aide from the lochan on Druim Coire nan Laogh.*

34. Mam na Cloich' Airde, the pass from Glen Dessarry to Loch Nevis.

the slopes of these mountains are more gradual and lead down to the forests on the south side of Loch Garry. The Cam Bhealach, a pass rising to about 610 m between Loch Lochy and the head of Gleann Cia-aig, divides the Loch Lochy hills into two roughly equal halves.

Meal na Teanga (917 m), Meall Coire Lochain (900 m), Meall Dubh (837 m)

The highest hill in the southern half is Meall na Teanga, flanked on the south by Meall Coire Lochain and on the north-east by Meall Dubh. The shortest approach to these hills is from Clunes. To avoid any bushwhacking through the closely planted trees of the Clunes Forest, follow the forest road shown on the Ordnance Survey map, north-east and then back west-south-west to its ending near the upper edge of the forest 1 km south of Leac Chorrach. From the road end scramble up a steep bank for a few metres and emerge onto the open hillside which leads, steeply at first, past Leac Chorrach and up the open grassy hillside to Meall Coire Lochain, whose summit is on the edge of a steep corrie. The ridge to Meall na Teanga drops steeply a few metres north of the cairn and is quite narrow and well-defined for 80 m down to the col from which the ascent to Meall na Teanga is straightforward. The top of this hill is near the south end of its level summit ridge. One can continue northwards down steep bouldery slopes to reach Meall Dubh or the Cam Bhealach.

An alternative route to Meall na Teanga from the south starts at the Eas Chia-aig waterfall at the west end of the Mile Dorcha ($2\frac{1}{2}$ km west of Clunes). Take the path through the forest on the east side of the stream for $\frac{1}{2}$ km and then strike up the hillside on the right to reach the forest road which goes up Gleann Cia-aig. This is followed for 3 km until one is beyond the forest and can climb eastwards up the steep grassy slopes of Meall Odhar and so along a pleasant ridge to Meall Coire Lochain.

Ben Tee (901 m)

The mountains in the northern half of the Loch Lochy group can be reached most easily from Laggan Locks or Kilfinnan farm. Ben Tee is a very prominent hill, its isolated cone being a feature of the landscape in this part of the Great Glen. It is easily climbed from Kilfinnan, taking the path on the north-east side of the Kilfinnan Burn and keeping well

F

up the hillside as one approaches the Kilfinnan Fall. (The more obvious lower path goes only a short distance and is apparently used by those going to view the Fall). Once on the level moorland north of the Fall one simply continues due west over rather featureless ground to the steeper and in places rocky cone of the summit. There is a rather indifferent path on the north side of the Allt a' Choire Ghlais above the Kilfinnan Fall, but it does not offer a quicker route to Ben Tee.

Sron a' Choire Ghairbh (935 m)

The highest of the Loch Lochy hills is Sron a' Choire Ghairbh, the summit of a long horseshoe ridge which faces north-east enclosing Coire Glas. The easiest ascent is from Kilfinnan, following the upper road through the South Laggan Forest for 3 km south-westwards and then climbing up the good path to the Cam Bhealach. From the top of the pass a stalker's path zig-zags up the hillside to the north for a further few hundred metres and ends just below the smooth mossy ridge a short distance from Sron a' Choire Ghairbh. The Coire Glas is a rather wild and remote corrie, but it has no great climbing interest. On the other side of the mountain the north and west slopes are uniformly steep and grassy, and quite featureless. An alternative route to the one just described from Kilfinnan is to follow the east ridge all the way over Meall nan Dearcag and Sean Mheall, but this is rougher going with a good deal of up and downhill along the ridge.

The circuit of Ben Tee and Sron a' Choire Ghairbh is a good hill-walk, Kilfinnan being the best starting and finishing point, but there is some very rough ground on the descent to the col between the two hills and the reascent on the other side. These two hills can also be climbed from Greenfield in Glen Garry, following the roads and paths through the Glengarry Forest and finally climbing them by their north-west slopes. Needless to say, the finest day of all in these hills is the traverse from Kilfinnan to Clunes over all the tops from Ben Tee to Meall Coire Lochain. It is perfectly feasible, particularly if one has a co-operative chauffeur.

Geal Charn (804 m), Meall na h-Eilde (838 m)

The country immediately to the west of the Loch Lochy hills is characterised by several rounded hills of 600 to 800 m height. Glas

Bheinn (732 m) and Geal Charn can both be easily climbed from Achnasaul on the north side of Loch Arkaig by the path up the Allt Dubh. To their north the line of hills Meall Tarsuinn (660 m), Meall Coire na Saobhaidh (820 m), Meall na h-Eilde and Meall an Tagraidh (761 m) can be traversed equally well from Achnasaul or from Greenfield.

The Glen Kingie–Glen Dessarry hills form a long range starting at Gairich near the east end of Loch Quoich and extending westwards on the south side of that loch for about 15 km to end at Sgurr na Ciche which, although it is only 3 km from the west coast at the head of Loch Nevis, stands on the east–west watershed of the Western Highlands. In its 15 km length this range shows a complete change of character from the smooth grassy dome of Gairich to the sharp-pointed, rock girt summit of Sgurr na Ciche and its even rougher neighbour Ben Aden. With the exception of Gairich, all the mountains in this group can be most easily climbed from the road end beyond the head of Loch Arkaig. Gairich, however, is usually climbed from the east end of Loch Quoich.

Sgurr Mhurlagain (879 m), Fraoch Bheinn (858 m), Druim a' Chuirn (815 m)

In addition to the range just noted, there are three lower hills on the south side of Glen Kingie which overlook the head of Loch Arkaig and Glen Dessarry. Sgurr Mhurlagain can be climbed easily from any point on the Loch Arkaig road near Murlaggan cottage; the south side of the hill up which one climbs is grassy and rather featureless, but the north side has a bit more character. Fraoch Bheinn is a fine little hill which is probably best climbed by its south ridge, starting at Strathan and climbing up the west side of the Dearg Allt. (It is easier but probably longer to take the path up this stream). The north-east ridge is an interesting line of ascent which can be recommended if one is coming up from Kinbreack in Glen Kingie. The third hill in this little group, Druim a' Chuirn is most easily climbed by the ridge rising above Glendessarry Lodge, and the traverse can be continued westwards along the narrow ridge to Sgurr Cos na Breachd-laoidh; the north side of this ridge above Glen Kingie is precipitous, and on the east side of Druim a' Chuirn, above the Feith a' Chicheanais, there are some fine rough slabs set at an easy angle which can provide some pleasant discontinuous scrambling. These hills are all short climbs, half a day each at the most, but they command good views of the higher hills to the north across Glen Kingie, and south-westwards towards Sgurr Thuilm.

There are stalkers' paths on both the east and west sides of Fraoch Bheinn which lead from Glen Dessarry to Kinbreack in Glen Kingie. They provide the shortest route to that bothy, and also a possible approach route to some of the mountains on the north side of Glen Kingie, however it is worth bearing in mind when planning any route which involves crossing the River Kingie that it is likely to be impassable during and after very wet weather. At the time of writing Kinbreack bothy is in quite good condition and is a good base for climbing the Glen Kingie hills.

The range of mountains on the north side of Glen Kingie may be briefly described as follows:—Gairich (919 m) at the eastern end is rather an isolated hill with a low pass (about 360 m) to its west. Then the ridge rises steeply to Sgurr an Fhuarain (901 m) and continues with only a slight drop to about 720 m before rising to Sgurr Mor (1003 m). There the ridge turns south-west and drops to 750 m before the peak of Sgurr Beag (890 m), down again to 660 m and up to An Eag (873 m), which stands close to the pass connecting the head of Glen Kingie to upper Glen Dessarry. Continuing westwards from An Eag, the ridge forms the watershed between Glen Dessarry and the streams draining northwards into Loch Quoich. The peaks on this ridge are Sgurr nan Coireachan (953 m), Garbh Chioch Mhor (1013 m) and finally Sgurr na Ciche (1040 m). From there the westward continuation of the ridge drops in 4 km to the head of Loch Nevis, but another ridge goes north-east to Meall a' Choire Dhuibh (740 m) overlooking the head of Loch Quoich, and then back west-north-west to Ben Aden (887 m). It is these mountains, from Gairich to Ben Aden, which form the main range in the area described in this chapter; it is one of the finest mountain ranges in the Western Highlands, becoming progressively wilder and rougher as one goes from east to west.

Gairich (919 m)

Gairich is most easily climbed from the east end of Loch Quoich, starting at the dam and following the path southwards over moorland to the point where it descends into the Glen Kingie forest. From there a good stalker's path climbs up the Druim na Geid Salaich and ends once level ground is reached on the broad crest of the ridge. The route continues westwards along this wide ridge until the steepening final slopes of Gairich are reached with the steep upper crags of Coire Thollaidh on one's right. Continue directly up, following a faint path (disregard the path which goes off to the left) and climbing a few short rocky steps to reach the mossy dome of the summit, crowned by a large cairn.

An alternative route to Gairich from the Glen Kingie side makes use of the path on the north side of the River Kingie opposite Kinbreack which climbs up to the pass, A'Mhaingir, west of the mountain. From the pass a stalker's path zig-zags steeply up the end of Gairich Beag, from where the ridge to Gairich itself is easy going.

Sgurr Mor (1003 m), Sgurr an Fhuarain (901 m), Sgurr Beag (890 m), An Eag (873 m)

Sgurr Mor, as its name implies, is a massive mountain, dominating the upper end of Loch Quoich and throwing down long uniformly steep slopes to Glen Kingie. It is rather inaccessible since the enlargement of Loch Quoich and the traditional route of ascent from the north is now open only to those with a canoe or dinghy in which to cross the loch. The usual route of ascent is, therefore, from the south, starting at Strathan, taking the path from Glendessarry Lodge over the pass west of Fraoch Bheinn and descending slightly to reach the headwaters of the River Kingie. After crossing the river (which at this high point should be possible even in the wettest of weather) one can either climb directly and tediously up the steep slope due north to the summit, or take a less direct route by the stalker's path onto the ridge south-west of Sgurr Beag. This path continues along the ridge to Sgurr Mor and makes the going very easy.

If one decides to spend a night at Kinbreack, and in doing so savour the great sense of solitude that pervades Glen Kingie, then a very good traverse can be made (assuming that the River Kingie is not in spate) by taking the path to Gairich for a couple of kilometres and then climbing Sgurr an Fhuarain by its east ridge. From there the path along the main ridge can be followed to Sgurr Mor and as far south-west as An Eag, from where one can either return down Glen Kingie to Kinbreack or descend to Glen Dessarry. In the latter case the first part of the descent from An Eag is south to the pass at the head of Glen Kingie. From there the walk down the Allt Coire nan Uth is not easy going as the corrie is very steep-sided and trackless. It may be better to face the short, steep climb from the pass to Sgurr Cos na Breachd-laoidh and then drop down the long easy-angled ridge to Glendessarry Lodge.

73

Sgurr nan Coireachan (953 m)

Sgurr nan Coireachan is a steep-sided mountain formed by a ridge running north to south. On the east side of the summit the Coire nan Uth has some impressive glaciated slabs high up. The most direct route of ascent is from Glen Dessarry by the steep grassy south ridge which rises directly above the footbridge over the Allt Coire nan Uth. A good circuit can be made by descending the rocky east ridge, climbing An Eag, and returning to Glendessarry Lodge as described in the preceding paragraph.

Garbh Chioch Mhor (1013 m)

The col immediately to the south-west of Sgurr nan Coireachan is the Bealach nan Gall, easily reached from Glen Dessarry by the stream flowing south from it. West of this col the main mountain ridge becomes much more rugged, with a great deal of outcropping rock, as it climbs to Garbh Chioch Bheag and continues to Garbh Chioch Mhor. There is a dry stone dyke of impressive proportions all the way along this ridge, a memorial and tribute to the toil of estate workers many years ago when landowners jealously staked out their territory. Nowadays hill-walkers may find this dyke of some route-finding help on days when the mist is very thick. The north side of the ridge drops steeply into Coire nan Gall in a succession of glaciated slabs, giving the upper part of this corrie a wild and craggy character. The south side of the ridge overlooking the watershed at the head of Glen Dessarry is steep, but less continuously rocky.

One simple route of ascent of Garbh Chioch Mhor from Glen Dessarry is up to the Bealach nan Gall and along the ridge, following the stone dyke all the way. The return can be varied by descending steeply north-west to the next col on the ridge, the Feadan na Ciche. From this col turn down south-west into Coire na Ciche until below the crags of Garbh Chioch Mhor, at which point one reaches a fairly level grassy terrace which can be traversed to the south-east until an easy descent leads down to the pass at the head of Glen Dessarry.

Sgurr na Ciche (1040 m)

One kilometre north-west of Garbh Chioch Mhor, across the rocky gap of the Feadan na Ciche, rises Sgurr na Ciche. This is the culminating peak of the great ridge that we have been following along the south side of Loch Quoich, and it is undoubtedly the finest. It rises as a solitary cone above its neighbours, and is the most prominent landmark in this area where the western extremity of Lochaber borders on Knoydart.

The mountain is formed by an 8 km long ridge running north-east from the head of Loch Nevis to the head of Loch Quoich, the summit itself being near the middle. The south-west ridge, called the Druim a' Ghoirtein, rises from the water's edge near Sourlies bothy in a series of steep steps and level sections with a final rocky rise to the summit. The north-east ridge rising from Loch Quoich is a good deal more rugged and it passes over the peak of Meall a' Choire Dhuibh. This ridge forms one of the enclosing walls of Coire nan Gall. On all sides of the summit the slopes are steep and rocky, and on the north-west side these slopes drop over a thousand metres to the River Carnach in a single sweep.

The most frequented routes of ascent of Sgurr na Ciche are from Glen Dessarry and from Loch Nevis. From Glen Dessarry, follow the path up the glen to the watershed and then climb north-west up the side of Garbh Chioch Mhor in a rising spiral traverse to reach the Feadan na Ciche, thus reversing the descent route described already. From the Feadan climb the final steep slope to the summit of Sgurr na Ciche as directly as the terrain permits. There is a narrow path which wends its way among the crags and boulders.

From the head of Loch Nevis the obvious route of ascent is the long south-west ridge, the Druim a' Ghoirtein. If one starts at Sourlies, this ridge is climbed in its entirety. If one starts at Camusrory or Carnoch, it is more convenient to climb up the steep grassy north flank of this ridge to reach its crest about mid-height.

A third route of ascent that was much used before the raising of Loch Quoich is the north-east ridge over Meall a' Choire Dhuibh, but now one has to walk about 10 km along the north side of Loch Quoich to reach the foot of the ridge, so this is a fairly strenuous expedition. There is a stalker's path at the foot of Coire nan Gall which climbs a short distance up the ridge, and it may be followed.

Ben Aden (887 m)

One last mountain in the area of this chapter remains to be described, Ben Aden. Despite the fact that it does not reach Munro status, Ben Aden is a superb peak which epitomises as well as any other the character of the Rough Bounds of Knoydart. It is steep and rocky on

75

all sides, and is linked to Meall a' Choire Dhuibh by a rough knobbly ridge. Practically any route up Ben Aden involves careful route-finding and possibly also some scrambling among its many crags; in misty weather it may be quite difficult to find an easy route, and this is particularly true of the descent, for the crags and cliffs are not well seen from above.

Probably the easiest route is from the Carnach River, starting at its junction with the Allt Achadh a' Ghlinne. Climb the south-west face of the mountain, keeping to the left (north) high up to avoid the steep rocks below the summit, and reach the north-west ridge. At the top of this ridge a couple of knolls or false tops are passed before the true summit is reached. The corrie at the head of the Allt Achadh a' Ghlinne is extraordinarily wild, hemmed in by crags, but there is a route up Ben Aden by the stream which tumbles down from the ridge $\frac{1}{2}$ km east of the summit.

The north face of the mountain overlooking Lochan nam Breac is if anything steeper and rockier than the south face, and it is certainly in a remoter setting. There is undeniably a challenge in climbing this, the remotest and steepest face of Ben Aden. There is a vast amount of good rough rock, granite pegmatite, to be climbed on the mountain, but little seems ever to have been done, and none recorded. The cliffs below the summit on the south-west face are quite large and in full view from Carnoch, so it is quite surprising that there are no records of any climbing there.

Walks and Paths

Loch Arkaig to Loch Nevis. This, the cross-country walker's trade route from Lochaber to Knoydart, has been described in the last chapter from Glen Dessarry as far as Sourlies bothy. Beyond there the best route for the next kilometre depends on the state of the tide. If it is out, then the easiest way is along the foreshore below a steep crag for $\frac{1}{2}$ km and then across the saltings north to the footbridge over the River Carnach. If the tide is in then one has to climb a short way up the hillside behind Sourlies and contour round on a narrow rough track before descending to the edge of the saltings. Once over the River Carnach one is in Knoydart, and the route to Inverie is over the Mam Meadail. There is a good path all the way, starting a short distance north of the ruins at Carnoch. (The whole path from Loch Arkaig to Inverie is a right-of-way) (27 km).

Loch Quoich to Loch Nevis. This route follows the northern boundary of the area described in this chapter. The starting point is where the road to Kinloch Hourn leaves Loch Quoich, and the first 10 km are along the lochside following in places the remains of old roads, most of which are now submerged. The crossing of the Abhainn Chosaidh may well be impossible if the burn is in spate. From the dam at the head of Loch Quoich the footpath to Lochan nam Breac is joined and followed for a short distance on the north side of the lochan before leaving the main path which goes to Barrisdale and taking an inferior and sometimes invisible path on the north side of the River Carnach. This was once a well made path, as can occasionally be seen, but all too often it disappears and there are sections of rough going in the steep-sided glen of the Carnach River, but the scenery is superb. Eventually one comes to fairly level ground and a better path below Ben Aden and Carnoch is reached across the level bog that once was cultivated land. This is a fine walk, but not all easy going (20 km).

Loch Arkaig to Glen Garry by Glen Kingie. From Strathan take the Dearg Allt path to Kinbreack, cross the River Kingie and follow the path on the north side of the glen below Gairich to Lochan where the Forestry Commission plantation is entered. At this point there is a choice of routes, either north to the Loch Quoich dam (18 km), or along the forest road on the north side of the River Kingie, crossing after a few kilometres and continuing to Loch Poulary and Glen Garry a few kilometres west of Tomdoun (22 km).

Loch Arkaig to Glen Garry by Gleann Cia-aig. From the waterfall a few hundred metres east of the foot of Loch Arkaig, take the path north through the forest on the east side of the stream for ½ km and keep uphill to join the forest road which is followed, becoming a path as far as the ruined cottage at the foot of Meall an Tagraidh. Cross the glen east to join the path which contours round the foot of Sron a' Choire Ghairbh, and follow this north into the Glengarry Forest, turning west to Greenfield and the bridge over Loch Garry (19 km), or east to White Bridge near Invergarry (21 km).

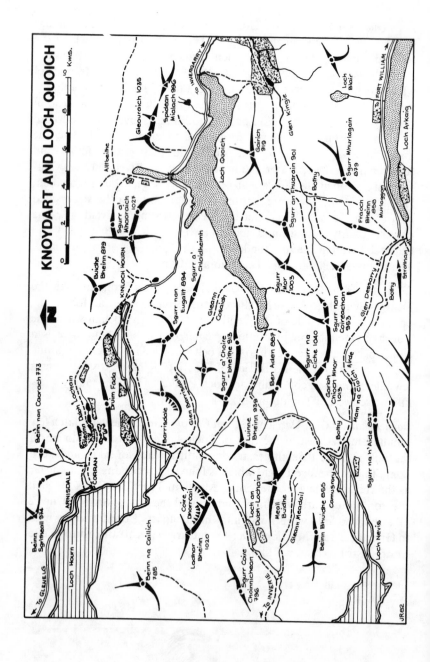

KNOYDART AND LOCH QUOICH

7

Knoydart

Sgurr nan Eugallt (894 m) 931045
Sgurr a' Choire-Bheithe (913 m) 895016
Luinne Bheinn (939 m) 868008
Meall Buidhe (946 m) 849990
Ladhar Bheinn (1020 m) 824041
Sgurr Coire Choinnichean (796 m) 790011
Beinn na Caillich (785 m) 796067
Beinn Bhuidhe (855 m) 822967

Munro's Tables, Section 10

MAPS: Ordnance Survey 1:50,000 (2nd Series) Sheet 33.

If one district in the Western Highlands epitomises better than any other the rugged grandeur and remoteness of this part of Scotland, then it must surely be Knoydart. This mountainous peninsula between the sea lochs Nevis and Hourn is one of the most inaccessible corners of the land, and the wild, rocky and inhospitable nature of much of the terrain well earns for itself the title The Rough Bounds of Knoydart. It is surrounded on three sides by the sea and long narrow sea lochs, and on the fourth side by the mountains around the north-west corner of Loch Quoich which make a very effective barrier, penetrated by a single narrow road and two footpaths.

From the mountaineer's point of view, Knoydart is best known for its three great mountains Ladhar Bheinn, Luinne Bheinn and Meall Buidhe, all Munros. There are, however, several other fine peaks which do not quite reach this status, and several good footpaths which are rights-of-way penetrate through the area. The two sea lochs which enclose Knoydart, Loch Nevis meaning the Loch of Heaven, and Loch Hourn meaning Hell's loch, are scenically two of the finest of Scotland's west coast lochs, being long, narrow and steeply enclosed by mountains. There is more than landscape, no matter how impressive, for the character of Knoydart is such that it is one of the most delectable goals in the Western Highlands for those in search of wilderness, solitude and adventure, whether it be in climbing the mountains, making long cross-country walks or sailing and canoeing round the coastline.

Inverie is the only habitation of any size in Knoydart. Its cottages and houses, the estate office and the shop are lined along the edge of Inverie Bay, looking out across the mouth of Loch Nevis towards the Inner Hebrides. The only public road in Knoydart is about 10 km long and links Inverie to the tiny village of Airor on the Sound of Sleat. Elsewhere there are several isolated houses round the coast, some of them inhabited. Camusrory at the head of Loch Nevis is occupied from time to time, at present during summer months by the Outward Bound School, Locheil. At Barrisdale on the north coast of Knoydart facing Loch Hourn a keeper is in residence all year.

One of the features that give Knoydart its distinctive character is that there is no road access into the district. The nearest road is at Kinloch Hourn, and that is on the north-eastern edge of Knoydart. Access to Inverie is by boat and there is a regular service from Mallaig three days a week. The times of sailings are published in the Highlands and Islands Development Board's Comprehensive Guide of Transport Services, and may also be found from the operator, Bruce Watt Cruises, Mallaig (Telephone 0687 2233). As mentioned in an earlier chapter, the Ordnance Survey map is inaccurate in showing that this service goes to the head of Loch Nevis. There is no regular boat service beyond Inverie, and anyone wishing to sail from Mallaig to the head of Loch Nevis would have to make special arrangements with a boat operator at Mallaig. The keeper at Barrisdale has a boat which he uses for communication with Arnisdale (Corran) and Kinloch Hourn, and if contacted beforehand he may be willing to provide sailings to and from Barrisdale. It may also be possible to arrange with a boatman at Arnisdale or Corran for a trip across Loch Hourn.

With the exception of the regular service between Mallaig and Inverie, none of these sailings can be relied on, and that leaves walking as possibly the most certain way of reaching Knoydart. The shortest approach is from the road end at Kinloch Hourn along 10 km of very pleasant path on the south side of Loch Hourn to Barrisdale. The alternatives are the much longer walks described in the preceding chapters from Loch Arkaig or Loch Quoich to the head of Loch Nevis, and from there over the Mam Meadail to Inverie.

Owners of canoes or lightweight dinghies will find that these forms of transport are ideal for making the journey from Kinloch Hourn to

Barrisdale. The upper end of Loch Hourn is superb, seals are often seen and the tiny rocky island Eilean Mhogh-sgeir has a heronry. However, both Barrisdale Bay and Loch Beag at the head of Loch Hourn dry out at low water, and the tide races through Caolas Mor, so it is necessary to choose the correct state of the tide before setting sail.

Accommodation in and around Knoydart is not plentiful. The keeper at Barrisdale has in recent years made available the bothy next to his house for visiting climbers and walkers outwith the stalking season. The bothy at Sourlies is a good base for climbing in the south-east corner of Knoydart, but it is rather far from Ladhar Bheinn. In recent years a bothy has been available at Kinloch Hourn, and at Inverie there is a hostel, intended for the use of estate workers, but also available to visiting climbers for a modest charge. Camping is of course possible, but permission is required to camp near Barrisdale and in the neighbour-hood of Inverie and in the glen of the Inverie River. (Anyone intending to visit Inverie and wishing to stay in the hostel or camp nearby is advised to contact the Factor of the Knoydart Estate in Inverie, Telephone 0687 2331). Elsewhere in Knoydart, wild camping in the truest sense of the word is probably the best solution to the accommodation problem.

It is appropriate at this stage to describe some of the principal footpaths in Knoydart as they are the key to travel in this area, and are useful approach routes to several of the mountains.

The path from Kinloch Hourn to Barrisdale has already been mentioned. Its continuation to Inverie goes south from Barrisdale, climbing steadily to the Mam Barrisdale (450 m), the important pass on the ridge between Luinne Bheinn and Ladhar Bheinn. The descent south-west to Gleann an Dubh-Lochain is steep at first, and at the lochan, where there is a fish farm, the path becomes a road for the rest of the way to Inverie (24 km from Kinloch Hourn).

The path from the head of Loch Nevis to Inverie (which is the last part of the right-of-way from Loch Arkaig to Inverie) starts at Carnoch and climbs in a series of well graded curves to the Mam Meadail (550 m). On the west side of this pass the path descends gradually into Gleann Meadail and joins the road in the Inverie glen near the prominent monument on Torr a' Bhalbhain, 3 km from Inverie. (28 km from the west end of Loch Arkaig).

There are two paths from Loch Quoich to Barrisdale, but the eastern ends of these paths must be reached by walking along the (in places) trackless shore of the loch from the nearest point on the Kinloch Hourn road. The first path leads up Gleann Cosaidh and down Glen Barrisdale, traversing very wild country on the north side of the little mountain Slat Bheinn. The Abhainn Chosaidh may be impossible to cross in spate near its outflow. The second path was once the main route from Kinloch Quoich to Barrisdale before the raising of the level of Loch Quoich. Now the path starts at the little dam at its west end goes along the south side of the burn flowing into Lochan nam Breac before crossing to the north side of the lochan. From there the path climbs in a series of well engineered gradients to the Mam Unndalain (550 m), and descends Gleann Unndalain to Barrisdale (19 km from the road at Loch Quoich). This path, along with others in Knoydart, was made many years ago by an engineer named James Watt who returned to Scotland from Rhodesia under a cloud and sought employment out of the public eye. He obtained a contract to link the glens in Knoydart, which he did very effectively with the help of only two men.

The path from the head of Loch Quoich to the head of Loch Nevis has been described in the previous chapter.

Sgurr nan Eugallt (894 m), Sgurr a' Choire-bheithe (913 m)

The eastern part of Knoydart is the Barrisdale Estate, and it consists principally of two very large mountains which just fail to reach Munro height. They are Sgurr nan Eugallt and Sgurr a' Choire-bheithe. Both are long ridges running roughly east to west, separated by Gleann Cosaidh, and both have numerous minor tops and bumps along their crests which are about 7 km long.

Sgurr nan Eugallt is the more accessible of the two as it overlooks the road from Loch Quoich to Kinloch Hourn in a series of rough corries. It was through one of these, Coire Bheithe, that Prince Charles in July 1746 broke through the cordon of Hanoverian troops that was trying to cut off his escape eastwards from the coast. With his party of five companions he crossed the east end of the Sgurr nan Eugallt ridge in darkness and descended the north-east side of the mountain, slipping past the Hanoverian sentries near Loch Coire Shubh before heading north to Glen Shiel and Affric.

The most straightforward route to Sgurr nan Eugallt is the stalker's path which starts at the ruined roadside cottäge of Coireshubh. This path ends just below the north-east ridge of the peak and this ridge is followed to the top. A good long traverse can now be enjoyed by going 1 km north-west to Sgurr Sgiath Airigh (881 m), and then retracing one's steps south-east along the ridge over many little tops to Sgurr a' Chlaidheimh (840 m) and beyond before descending into Coire Bheithe.

Sgurr a' Choire-bheithe is rather less accessible from the east, being a long walk from the nearest point on the road along the side of Loch Quoich. Two shorter routes of ascent are therefore the path from Barrisdale to the Mam Unndalain and then steeply uphill to reach the ridge a short distance west of the summit, and secondly the path from the head of Loch Nevis up the River Carnach until one is below the south side of the peak, and then directly and steeply uphill. The summit is at the west end of the long ridge called the Druim Chosaidh which forms the spine of the mountain. The traverse of this ridge is a very fine walk with plenty of up and downhill work over the many little tops, and even some scrambling if one stays right on the crest of the ridge.

An Caisteal (610 m), Meall nan Eun (666 m)

Four kilometres west of Sgurr nan Eugallt there are two small rocky hills on the north side of Glen Barrisdale, An Caisteal and Meall nan Eun. With the lower hill Carn Mairi, which rises directly above Barrisdale House, they enclose a little corrie above Loch Hourn. The north face of An Caisteal is slabby, about 200 m high and set at an angle of 45°. In the centre of the face there is a very clean continuous sweep of slabs extending virtually the whole height of the face. To the left and right of this central area the slabs are less continuous, and intersected by grassy ledges and grooves. The central area of slabs gives excellent climbing reminiscent of the Etive Slabs, and three routes have been recorded, one on the left edge of the slabs, one fairly directly up the middle and one on the right. Pitons were required for belays. Brief details of these three routes are:—

Portcullis (205 m, Very Severe) by I. S. Clough and B. Rex (1967) follows a fairly direct line up the left edge of the central sweep of slabs except for a grassy diversion leftwards near the top.

In 1980 B. McMillan and G. Strange climbed the central sweep of slabs by a fairly direct line, passing just right of the obvious wet break in the upper overhangs (180 m, Very Severe).

Battlement Slab (195 m, Very Severe) starts just right of the toe of the slabs and appears to be to the right of the previous route, i.e. keeping to the right side of the slabs.

(Detailed descriptions of Portcullis and Battlement Slab are in S.M.C.J., Vol. XXIX, No. 159, pp. 60–61).

The west face of Meall nan Eun is much less impressive, consisting of easy-angled buttresses of no great distinction. One exception to this might be the little buttress immediately below the Meall nan Eun—An Caisteal col, which is quite steep and whose upper part has a distinctively rounded appearance. Two routes have been made on this buttress by K. Schwartz and Miss M. Horsburgh in 1971. *Parapet* (90 m, Severe) is on the edge facing down the corrie, the only difficulty being a short vertical step near the top. *Bastion* (90 m, Hard Severe) is on the steep right wall, the start being indicated by an arrow. (S.M.C.J., Vol. XXX, No. 165, p. 271).

Going leftwards (north) from this buttress across the grassy slope leading up to the col, there are two small buttresses, each about 100 m high, and further left a larger buttress formed by rocky ribs with a prominent slab high up. These three buttresses have all been climbed by routes of not more than Difficult standard, and require no description (S.M.C.J., Vol. XXIX, No. 159, p. 61 and Vol. XXX, No. 165, p. 271).

Luinne Bheinn (939 m), Meall Buidhe (946 m)

The centre of Knoydart is dominated by the two mountains Luinne Bheinn and Meall Buidhe which together extend across the peninsula from the head of Loch Nevis to Barrisdale. They are very rough, craggy mountains, though nowhere are there cliffs of any great size or height. One of their most interesting features is the Coire Odhair on the west side of their connecting ridge; this corrie has a very fine display of glaciated rock, with two little lochans lying in its depths.

Luinne Bheinn consists of a narrow ridge running west from the Mam Unndalain to the double topped summit, and then dropping north-west to the Mam Barrisdale. The north and south sides of the summit ridge are very steep and there is a fine corrie, the Coire Glas, on the north side overlooking Barrisdale. The true summit is the west top, marked by a small cairn, with a larger cairn a short distance along the north-west ridge. When descending southwards from Luinne Bheinn it is advisable not to go down directly south from the summit as the side of the ridge drops very steeply in broken cliffs. It is better to go a short distance west then descend south by a grassy gully for about 100 m to reach the top of a broad grassy shelf which drops at an easy angle towards the col at the head of Coire Odhair.

Meall Buidhe has two tops, the western one being the higher. The east top is at the edge of a steep little crag on the north face of the mountain, and stands at the junction of its three ridges. The west ridge

35.	In the Great Glen near Fort Augustus, looking south-west to the Loch Lochy and Glen Garry hills.

36.	In Glen Garry, looking towards Ben Tee and Sron a' Choire Ghairbh.

37. *Gairich from Glen Garry.*

38. *Gairich, Sgurr an Fhuarain and Sgurr Mor from the north-east.*

39.   Sourlies bothy at the head of Loch Nevis.

40.   Ben Aden from Carnoch.

41. *Looking west along Loch Quoich to Sgurr Mor (left), Sgurr na Ciche and Ben Aden (right).*

42.   On the ridge of Garbh Chioch Mhor, looking north-west to Sgurr na Ciche.

43.   Ben Aden and Sgurr na Ciche from Camusrory at the head of Loch Nevis.

44. *Sgurr na Ciche from Mam Meadail.*

drops 4 km to the junction of the Inverie River and the Allt Gleann Meadail. The south-east ridge drops over Sgurr Sgeithe towards Carnoch, and the north-east ridge goes round the head of Coire Odhair to link Meall Buidhe to Luinne Bheinn, and these two last named ridges enclose a fine little corrie at the head of the Allt na Sealga where steep slabby rocks plunge down to a tiny lochan.

These two mountains are often climbed together, and will be described accordingly. Being in the centre of Knoydart, they are equally accessible from Inverie, Barrisdale and the head of Loch Nevis. The approach from Loch Quoich in the east is much longer.

From Inverie take the route to the Mam Barrisdale and climb Luinne Bheinn by its north-west ridge. Descend southwards by the route described above and traverse round the head of Choire Odhair; the ridge round the corrie climbs over the top of Druim Leac a' Shith, and this little bit of climbing can be avoided by traversing along fairly obvious grass terraces on the west side of the ridge to reach the Bealach Ile Coire. From this bealach Meall Buidhe is climbed by its north-east ridge, which becomes steeper and narrower as it approaches the top. The descent is down the west ridge which is pleasantly easy going; it is probably best, especially in wet weather, to aim for the footbridge across the Allt Gleann Meadail.

From Barrisdale take the path up Gleann Unndalain to the Mam Unndalain and climb the east ridge of Luinne Bheinn. Traverse to Meall Buidhe as above. The return journey is best made by descending the easy gully north-east from the col between the two tops of Meall Buidhe into Choire Odhair, aiming for the two lochans amid grand rock scenery. From the lochans traverse north, at first across the steep side of Luinne Bheinn and then more easily to the Mam Barrisdale, and so back to Barrisdale.

From Carnoch the route follows the path to the Mam Meadail, then steeply uphill north to reach Meall Buidhe's south-east ridge which is followed easily to the top. Traverse round Choire Odhair to Luinne Bheinn from where the easiest return to Carnoch is along the summit ridge to the east peak and then steeply downhill south-east to the River Carnach.

Ladhar Bheinn (1020 m)

Ladhar Bheinn (pronounced Larven) is the finest mountain in Knoydart, arguably the finest in the Western Highlands, and in most people's list of the best dozen in Scotland. It is a complex mountain of several ridges,

G

peaks and corries, but its heart and the centre of climbing interest is the horseshoe of ridges and peaks that enclose Coire Dhorrcail. This corrie, facing north-east to Loch Hourn, is one of the finest in the Highlands with great cliffs along its headwall and its south-east side in the smaller Coire na Cabaig. The summit of Ladhar Bheinn is near the western corner of Coire Dhorrcail, which is the meeting point of three ridges. The summit cairn is on the west-north-west ridge a short distance from the junction, the north-east ridge drops and rises again over the peak of Stob a' Choire Odhair (960 m) and forms one arm enclosing Coire Dhorrcail; the south-east ridge, which forms the headwall of the corrie, drops to the Bealach Coire Dhorrcail and rises to Stob a' Chearcaill (849 m) whose ridge runs at right angles to it forming a well defined T. The north-east ridge of Stob a' Chearcaill drops very steeply at first and then continues to Creag Bheithe above Barrisdale Bay; the south-west ridge, called the Aonach Sgoilte, goes for several kilometres to end at the sharp pointed peak of Sgurr Coire Choinnichean above Inverie. The complete traverse of this ridge from Barrisdale to Inverie or vice versa is a fine expedition, probably seldom done.

Altogether Ladhar Bheinn is a complex and magnificent mountain. Its only dull feature is the south-west side above Gleann na Guiserein. The north part of the mountain, Coire Each and Coire Odhar, are very wild and seldom visited, being off the climber's normal routes. There is a magnetic anomaly on Ladhar Bheinn, and the magnetic compass is not reliable.

The classic traverse of Ladhar Bheinn is the circuit of Coire Dhorrcail, which is best done from Barrisdale. Take the stalker's path to Coire Dhorrcail and at the point where it crosses the lower part of the Creag Bheithe ridge turn left and climb this ridge. As one gains height there are superb views towards Ladhar Bheinn, and in due course the ridge abuts against the steep peak of Stob a' Chearcaill. The ascent directly up this peak is quite a scramble, traversing to and fro on grassy ledges and climbing short pitches, however with good route-finding there are no great difficulties. It would certainly be more difficult to find the right route in mist, or in descent, and it is possible to find an easier route of ascent by traversing round to the south-east for a short distance before climbing up. An alternative, but less fine route to Stob a' Chearcaill is by the Mam Barrisdale and the south-east face of the peak. The last part of this route to the summit ridge is also quite steep, but with good route-finding an easy way can be found. Once on Stob a' Chearcaill its fine ridge is followed past the tops of two or three impressively steep gullies, and at Pt 849 m one turns north-west and descends the broad ridge to Bealach Coire Dhorrcail. Near the bealach a prominent spur juts out into Coire Dhorrcail, separating that corrie from the smaller Coire na Cabaig, and there is quite an easy descent northwards from the bealach down steep grass; this is probably the easiest route of ascent or descent in the whole cirque of Coire Dhorrcail. The ascent to Ladhar Bheinn continues along the headwall of the corrie, over the tops of several buttresses and descending slightly between them to look down into the depths of dark gullies. Eventually the last of these clefts is passed, a steep climb leads to the junction of the ridges, and the summit is a short distance along the nearly level ridge to the west. Returning to the junction, the north-east ridge is descended quite steeply and there is a short reascent to the narrow peak of Stob a' Choire Odhair, from where there is a particularly fine view down to Barrisdale Bay, and beyond it towards the head of Loch Hourn. Continuing the descent, the ridge becomes broad and grassy with a few small crags, and one can leave it and descend east into the lower part of Coire Dhorrcail to the start of the stalker's path back to Barrisdale.

The ascent from Inverie is a lot longer. One route, hardly worthy of the mountain, is to take the path north from the pier over the Mam Uidhe into Gleann na Guiserein and climb the south-west side of Ladhar Bheinn, a steep but rather uninteresting ascent. A better way is to follow the road up the Inverie River to the outflow of Loch an Dubh-Lochain, then climb north to Mam Suidheig and traverse the ridge east-north-east to Aonach Sgoilte and the 849 m top of Stob a' Chearcaill, where the Barrisdale route is joined.

The climbing possibilities of the great cliffs of Coire Dhorrcail were recognised long ago, probably as early as the celebrated S.M.C. yachting meet of Easter 1897. In the following year H. Raeburn and his companions made the first ascent of the prominent gully at the centre of the cliffs which now bears his name. It was realised that the unfavourable strata of the rock and the profuse vegetation made the cliffs quite unsuitable for summer rock-climbing, and that the best possibilities would be in winter; however, the remoteness of Ladhar Bheinn and its proximity to the west coast made winter climbing problematical. Many years elapsed, with at least one unsuccessful attempt to climb one of the gullies of Stob a' Chearcaill, until finally in 1963 T. Patey and his companions climbed two fine gullies, *Viking* and *Gaberlunzie*, and revived interest in the winter climbing potential of the mountain. In the last twenty years other climbers have followed, and ten routes have been recorded in the S.M.C. Journal, all of them done in winter. The description which follows refers to winter conditions.

The main feature of the Coire Dhorrcail cliffs is the very large buttress about 350 m high at their left hand end, not far from the Bealach Coire Dhorrcail. In winter the centre of this buttress usually holds a big steep snowfield, with an icy groove below it and icy grooves reaching upwards from its upper edge. The similarity to the White Spider on the North Face of the Eiger is remarkable, hence the name *Spider Buttress* for this great feature of the mountain. Two ribs or smaller buttresses enclose the central snowfield, the East and West pillars. To the right of *Spider Buttress* is the long curving *Viking Gully*, its many ice pitches concealed until one is directly below the gully. Continuing right there are two lesser buttresses (very grassy in summer) separated by a big gully. Next is *Raeburn's Gully*, a prominent narrow cleft bounded on its right by the rounded *Landlubbers' Buttress*. Further right the cliffs become smaller, about 200 m high, and they are characterised by a series of grooves or corners above which a steep slope leads towards the summit. The following routes have been recorded:—

East Rib (350 m, Grade IV) C. Higgins and R. Speiss. This route follows the left-hand rib of Spider Buttress, starting at the lowest point and maintaining a central line as far as possible. (S.M.C.J., Vol. XXXI, No. 170, p. 409).

Eastern Chimney (270 m, Grade IV) D. Broadhead, S. Gallacher and D. Rubens. A thin fault line rises from a square-cut bay 90 m above the base of the East Pillar of Spider Buttress. The fault line eventually crosses the buttress high above the central snowfield. Follow the fault line, which is extremely narrow in places for 120 m to the crest of the East Pillar. Short walls and grooves lead in 60 m to easier ground and the ridge above. (S.M.C.J., Vol. XXXII, No. 171, p. 59).

Tir na Og (350 m, Grade V) A. Foster and C. Higgins. This route takes a direct central line up Spider Buttress. Climb into the central snowfield by icy grooves, directly up the snowfield to central groove above and up this groove to its end just left of the summit of the buttress. (S.M.C.J., Vol. XXXI, No. 170, p. 409).

West Pillar (350 m, Grade III) D. Dinwoodie and A. McIvor. This is the right-hand rib of Spider Buttress. The icefall below the central snowfield is turned on the left, then a diagonal ascent of the snowfield rightwards leads to a snow ramp leading onto the crest of the West Pillar which is followed to the top. (S.M.C.J., Vol. XXXI, No. 169, p. 279).

Face Route (350 m, Grade III/IV) A. Nisbet and P. Tipton. This route is not far from the previous one. From the top right hand corner of the central snowfield the right hand of two grooves is climbed leading towards the West Pillar. Before reaching the crest of the pillar an obvious line rising parallel to the crest is followed to the summit. (S.M.C.J., Vol. XXXI, No. 169, p. 280).

Viking Gully (350 m, Grade III/IV) T. W. Patey and A. G. Nicol. This long curving gully has a succession of 15–20 m ice pitches in the middle part of the gully. (S.M.C.J., Vol. XXVII, No. 154, p. 374).

Raeburn's Gully (250 m, Grade III) H. Raeburn and party. The principal difficulty is a 30 m pitch rather less than half way up which on the first ascent was turned by climbing on the left.

Landlubbers' Buttress (250 m, Grade IV) A. Nisbet and P. Tipton. This is the slabby buttress right of Raeburn's Gully. Climb the left side of the buttress to a rock band. Go to a prominent flake on the right skyline, pass it and go back left via a snowy groove. Continue diagonally left past next rock band to reach snow ledge, make a descending traverse left across a slab (crux on first ascent) to reach an easy ramp which leads back to the crest of the buttress. Scramble to the top. (S.M.C.J., Vol. XXXI, No. 169, p. 280).

Summit Route (250 m, Grade III) A. Foster and C. Higgins. There are two prominent stepped corners in the cliff at the top right hand corner of the corrie. This route is up the right one. Climb snow and ice to belay left of an ice-fall. Traverse right and climb a series of grooves until a traverse right can be made above an ice-fall. Continue up snowfield.

Transatlantic Bong (200 m, Grade IV) C. Higgins and K. Sims. The left-hand of the two stepped corners.

Thunderchicken (200 m, Grade III) C. Higgins and K. Sims. The first corner to the left of the two stepped corners. (S.M.C.J., Vol. XXXI, No. 170, p. 409 for the last three routes).

The north-west face of Stob a' Chearcaill is about 250 m high and very steep, its appearance reminiscent of the north face of the Grandes Jorasses. There are several well-defined buttresses and gullies, but only the latter have attracted attention.

Gaberlunzie Gully (250 m, Grade III/IV) A. G. Nicol, R. W. P. Barclay and T. W. Patey. This is the main central gully. Above a small snow fan the lower 60 m is steep and gives 30 m of hard climbing up a snow channel leading to a chockstone which on the first ascent was overcome on the left. The angle eases and there are no difficulties until the final 60 m where the gully becomes an ice runnel. The last 20 m up the right-hand enclosing wall is perhaps the hardest part of the climb. (S.M.C.J., Vol. XXVII, No. 154, p. 374).

Para Handy Gully (250 m, Grade III) A. Ewing and W. Sproul. This is the prominent gully to the left of Gaberlunzie. It is at a continuously steep angle, and the entrance and exit are the hardest parts of the climb. (S.M.C.J., Vol. XXX, No. 165, p. 271).

Sgurr Coire Choinnichean (796 m), Beinn na Caillich (785 m), Beinn Bhuidhe (855 m)

Finally, before leaving Knoydart, mention may be made of three lesser, but by no means insignificant peaks. Sgurr Coire Choinnichean is the sharply pointed peak rising directly above Inverie which looks so impressive as one approaches the village by boat from Mallaig. The ascent direct from Inverie is very steep, but should present no problems. To avoid the forest behind the village it is best to follow the road up the Inverie glen for a kilometre or so before striking uphill towards Coire na Cloiche and the south-west end of the narrow upper ridge of the peak.

Beinn na Caillich is a rather remote hill, and quite a long walk from Inverie. Take the path over the Mam Uidhe to Gleann na Guiserein and climb the southern shoulder of the hill. In wet weather it will probably be necessary to go upstream in Gleann na Guiserein in order to cross the river.

Beinn Bhuidhe is the massive hill which commands the whole of the north side of Loch Nevis beyond Kylesknoydart. It can be climbed by the long undulating ridge from the Mam Meadail, or directly from the loch-side near Camusrory, making a rising traverse across the steep hillside. The Ordnance Survey map is misleading in its indication of a Mountain Rescue Post at Camusrory. There is, at the time of writing, no more than a casualty bag, and certainly not a complete set of rescue equipment. In winter Camusrory is not occupied, and any climbers involved in an accident in this area would have to seek help at Inverie.

8

Loch Quoich to Glen Shiel

Spidean Mialach (996 m) 066043
Gleouraich (1035 m) 040054
Sgurr a' Mhaoraich (1027 m) 984065
Creag a' Mhaim (947 m) 088077
Druim Shionnach (987 m) 074084
Aonach air Chrith (1021 m) 051083
Maol Chinn-dearg (981 m) 032088
Sgurr an Doire Leathain (1010 m) 015100
Sgurr an Lochain (1004 m) 005104
Creag nan Damh (918 m) 983112
Sgurr a' Bhac Chaolais (885 m) 958110
Sgurr na Sgine (945 m) 946113
The Saddle (1010 m) 935131
Beinn Sgritheall (974 m) 836126
Beinn na h-Eaglaise (804 m) 854120
Beinn nan Caorach (773 m) 871122

Munro's Tables, Section 10

MAPS: Ordnance Survey 1:50,000 (2nd Series) Sheets 33 and 34.

This is another well-defined slice of West Highland territory, the southern boundary being Glen Garry, Loch Quoich and Loch Hourn, and the northern boundary Glen Moriston, Loch Cluanie, Glen Shiel and Loch Duich. As is the case with several other areas described in this guide book, it can be divided into two parts, an eastern section which is of no great interest to the climber, and the rest which is of considerable climbing interest. The dividing line is the main road (A87) from the south to Kyle of Lochalsh which crosses the high moorland between Glen Garry and Glen Moriston. To the east of this road there is an extensive tract of rough country rising at its highest to Meall Dubh (788 m), and there are large areas of forest near Fort Augustus and on the hillsides above Loch Ness and Glen Moriston.

West of the Kyle road, however, the landscape is very different, and one has only to stop at one of the roadside parking places near the top of the hill above Loch Garry to appreciate one of the great West Highland panoramas. Many of the mountains described in the last two chapters are there along the horizon, and to the north of them, round the head of Loch Loyne, are some of the mountains of this chapter.

On the north side of Loch Quoich there are three fine hills, Spidean Mialach, Gleouraich and Sgurr a' Mhaoraich. To their north, over-looking Strath Cluanie and Glen Shiel, is the South Glen Shiel Ridge, a splendid ridge about 14 km long with seven Munros. Beyond their western end, and really part of the same chain of mountains, are Sgurr na Sgine and The Saddle. Further to the west there is the broad peninsula between Loch Duich and Loch Hourn where the solitary Beinn Sgritheall towers over the little village of Arnisdale on Loch Hourn.

The mountains in this area are all very accessible, none of them being more than about 4 km from the nearest road. The main route of access is of course the A87 and its branch westwards past Tomdoun to Kinloch Hourn. The other branch road which leaves the A87 at Shiel Bridge, crosses the Mam Ratagan pass and goes to Glenelg and Arnisdale and almost completes the circuit of this peninsula, leaving only the head of Loch Hourn for the walker.

On the south side of the area there are hotels at Invergarry and Tomdoun, and a camp and caravan site at Faichem just west of Invergarry. In the north the hotel at Cluanie is right in the heart of the mountains, a traditional mountaineers' inn. At the foot of Glen Shiel there are hotels, and no lack of cottages and houses offering bed and breakfast. The youth hostel at Ratagan is one of the SYHA's oldest and most popular, and there is a camp and caravan site at Shiel Bridge. On the far side of the Mam Ratagan, there is a small inn at Glenelg, and in that village and at Arnisdale there are bed and breakfasts and cottages to let. Throughout the area described in this chapter wild camping is possible, provided discretion is used, and for the bothy dweller there is the lonely cottage at Suardalan on the west side of the forest in Glen More.

For those without their own transport some useful bus services can be used to reach this area. There are the Glasgow–Fort William–Kyle of Lochalsh service on all weekdays throughout the year, the Edinburgh–Fort William–Kyle of Lochalsh service on Saturdays only in summer, and the Inverness–Glen Moriston–Kyle of Lochalsh service on week-days all year. In addition there is a post-bus service from Invergarry to

Kinloch Hourn three days a week; this is a 4-seat Land Rover, so it would be advisable to enquire beforehand (Telephone Invergarry Post Office, 08093201). A similar service operates on weekdays between Kyle of Lochalsh, Shiel Bridge, Glenelg and Arnisdale, also using a 4-seat vehicle, so one should telephone 059-982 200 beforehand.

Spidean Mialach (996 m), Gleouraich (1027 m)

The first two mountains that one comes to in this area are Spidean Mialach and Gleouraich. They form a very fine ridge on the north side of Loch Quoich, and their traverse is a delightful expedition, giving all the pleasures of West Highland ridge-walking with the advantage (in some peoples' eyes) of a very short and easy approach. The south side of these mountains is mostly grassy with some scree high up; the north side is a contrast, with wild and rugged corries and rocky spurs above the head of Glen Loyne.

The traverse of the two mountains is most conveniently done by starting at the foot of the Allt Coire Peitireach, 4 km west of the Loch Quoich dam. A short distance along the road eastwards a rough track slants up the hillside as far as the electricity transmission line, and thereafter a good stalker's path continues as far as the headwaters of the Allt a' Mheil. From the end of this path one should climb east for 1 km up easy grassy slopes and then north-east to the summit of Spidean Mialach. The ridge westwards drops to the Fiar Bealach (742 m), and there is a good zig-zag stalker's path up the ridge to the east top of Gleouraich, called Craig Coire na Fiar Bhealaich (1006 m). A further drop and rise bring one to the main summit. The descent goes north-west at first, descending slightly to the junction of two ridges, and then south-west to reach the top of a stalker's path. This turns out to be an excellent path, giving an easy and enjoyable descent; for some distance the path goes along the south-west ridge on its west flank which is so steep that there is a feeling of exposure, with Loch Quoich a long way below. Lower, the path zig-zags down the grassy hillside to return to the road through a patch of overgrown rhododendrons, the only remaining signs of the gardens of the long-since flooded Glenquoich Lodge.

Another stalker's path goes from Alltbeithe in Glen Quoich up the north-west ridge of Gleouraich to a height of about 700 m, but this route of ascent or descent is rarely used.

Sgurr a' Mhaoraich (1027 m)

Sgurr a' Mhaoraich, the third of the trio of Munros on the north side of Loch Quoich, is separated from the other two by the 3 km long arm of Loch Quoich created by the raising of its level. With its two lower tops, Am Bathaich and Sgurr Thionail, it forms a large and isolated mountain. Seen from Loch Hourn, it seems to completely block the head of the loch with its great bulk. Like so many of the mountains in this area its south side is grassy, forming a big open corrie, the Coire nan Eiricheallach; the west and north sides of the mountain are a lot steeper and rockier, and the east face holds the steep-sided Coire a' Chaorainn.

A pleasant traverse of Sgurr a' Mhaoraich makes use of two good stalker's paths. One can start 1 km beyond the bridge over the arm of Loch Quoich and climb the path up the broad ridge on the east side of Coire nan Eiricheallach to Sgurr Coire nan Eiricheallach (891 m), and beyond to Sgurr a' Mhaoraich. The descent north leads down a very steep grass slope to the col at about 790 m, then a rocky ridge leads to Am Bathaich (c.910 m). Continuing east along a narrow ridge, one reaches the top of a stalker's path which zig-zags steeply down the grassy crest and leads to the private road to Alltbeithe. A walk of $3\frac{1}{2}$ km along this road brings one back to the day's starting point.

No doubt Sgurr a' Mhaoraich can be climbed by other routes on its south-west side, starting at various points on the Kinloch Hourn road, but there are no obvious well-defined ways except possibly the south ridge which if ascended due north from Loch a' Choire Bheithe is probably the shortest and quickest way to the summit.

Glen Quoich divides at Alltbeithe and its two halves, Easter and Wester Glen Quoich, form a deep valley running roughly east to west which with the head of Glen Loyne separate the three mountains just described from the next range to the north, the South Glen Shiel Ridge. A path from Alltbeithe goes up Wester Glen Quoich, following the line of an old drove road over the pass at its head, the Bealach Duibh Leac, and descends steeply on the north-west side to Glen Shiel. Another path starting at Loch Coire Shubh near Kinloch Hourn crosses the pass north-west of Sgurr a' Mhaoraich and joins the previous one in Wester Glen Quoich. These two paths provide walking routes from Loch Quoich or Kinloch Hourn to Glen Shiel, and taken together they could give an interesting walk circumnavigating Sgurr a' Mhaoraich on a day when the weather is too bad for the tops. It was by the route north from

Loch Coire Shubh to Wester Glen Quoich and Glen Shiel that Prince Charles escaped north-eastwards to Glen Moriston after breaking through the cordon of Hanoverian troops on his epic journey of July 1746.

The South Glen Shiel Ridge

The South Glen Shiel Ridge is one of the finest mountain ranges in the Western Highlands. It extends for about 14 km and includes seven Munros and two lesser peaks in its length. The drops between the individual peaks are not very great, only once does the ridge fall below 800 m. The seven Munros, going from east to west, are—**Creag a' Mhaim** (947 m), **Druim Shionnach** (987 m), **Aonach air Chrith** (1021 m), **Maol Chinn-dearg** (981 m), **Sgurr an Doire Leathain** (1010 m), **Sgurr an Lochain** (1004 m) and **Creag nan Damh** (918 m).

The south side of the ridge is steep and grassy along nearly its whole length, forming a continuous and rather monotonous hillside above Glen Quoich. One or two stalker's paths climb up this steep hillside, but the ascent to the ridge from the south is rather uninteresting and cannot be recommended. The north side of the ridge overlooking Glen Shiel is much more interesting as there are several fine corries and subsidiary ridges between them which give character and shape to the individual peaks.

The ridge itself is well-defined along its whole length, narrow in places, but never difficult. Route finding presents no problem for there are signs of a path the whole way, and lines of old iron fence posts in places. Even without these aids to navigation, the ridge is defined by steep grass slopes dropping on the south side, and the rockier headwalls of the northern corries on the other side. Its popularity is due to the pleasure of this long high-level walk, and the fact that one can climb seven Munros in a day that is not too long or strenuous, provided one has made suitable transport arrangements. It would be a pity to end such a fine day with a long road walk in Glen Shiel.

The traverse is probably best done from east to west. In this case start by walking up the old road from Cluanie to Tomdoun as far as the bridge over the Allt Giubhais, and then climb fairly directly southwards to the summit of Creag a' Mhaim. The ridge westwards is broad as far as the col, but there is a narrow section leading up to Druim Shionnach, a rather flat-topped peak. The next 2 km of the ridge go along the top of Coire an t-Slugain, and there are some fine cliffs and gullies in the

95

headwall of this corrie. A fine feature of Aonach air Chrith is its north ridge, the Druim na Ciche. For a short distance from the summit this ridge is narrow and rocky, and gives some good scrambling as far as the little peak of A'Chioch, but this is a diversion enjoyed by few. Continuing west, the main ridge is quite narrow, but perfectly easy as far as Sgurr an Doire Leathain, whose summit is on a grassy spur about 100 m north of the main ridge. The next mountain, Sgurr an Lochain, is the most shapely of the seven, being a well-defined conical peak with a fine corrie on its east side holding the lochan which gives the mountain its name. The next top, Sgurr Beag, is probably bypassed by many for it is not a Munro and an easy traverse across its south flank saves a bit of climbing and also leads to a source of water which will be welcome on a hot day. The ridge continues down to its lowest col (726 m) and finally climbs to Creag nan Damh.

Two descent routes to Glen Shiel are possible: the shorter one goes north-east from the summit into Am Fraoch-choire, descending steeply to about 400 m to reach a stalker's path (not shown on the Ordnance Survey map) which leads down to Glen Shiel at a little plantation; alternatively, continue west from Creag nan Damh for 2 km to the Bealach Duibh Leac where the path described already is joined and followed down to Glen Shiel.

For those who do not want to traverse the whole ridge in a single day, there are two or three easy routes on the north side which lead down to Glen Shiel, and are equally good as ascent routes. The easiest of these, conveniently situated near the mid-point between Creag a' Mhaim and Creag nan Damh, is the north-east ridge of Maol Chinndearg which is very easy, and grassy in its lower part where there is a zig-zag stalker's path. This is not, however, the only route, and it is possible with due care to ascend or descend any of the ridges or corries on the north side of the South Glen Shiel Ridge.

The most impressive crags are probably those in Coire an t-Slugain, and there are at least two cliffs high up in the corrie which are characterised by the slabby appearance of their rocks. The easternmost of these crags is on the west face of Druim Shionnach in the south-east corner of Coire an t-Slugain, and it can most easily be approached by the west side of the north ridge of the peak to about the 900 m contour, followed by a short descending traverse south-west to the foot of the crag. The following route has been recorded on this crag:—

The Silver Slab (100 m, Severe) J. W. Haggas, S. Thompson and Miss P. B. White. Between a large gully in the centre of the crag and two large caves on the left, there are two buttresses separated by a smaller gully. The climb is on the left-hand of these two buttresses, starting to the left of a small chimney and going fairly directly up by slabs, cracks and occasional short traverses in pitches of 30, 25, 20, 15 and 10 m.

In addition to this route, there have been ascents (presumably in winter conditions) of gullies in both Coire an t-Slugain and Coire nan Eirecheanach on the west side of Aonach air Chrith. Sgurr an Lochain also looks as if there are one or two fine gullies in its eastern corrie which would be worth climbing in winter. It is surprising that there has been no record of any such ascents, for this corrie is well seen from the main road in Glen Shiel and looks very fine in winter.

The right-of-way from Glen Shiel to the Bealach Duibh Leac goes for 2 km up the Allt Mhalagain, and it is a good path as far as the crossing of the Allt Coire Toteil. Thereafter it becomes rather overgrown and more difficult to follow as it climbs steeply to the bealach. This path is not only a good route of access to the west end of the South Glen Shiel Ridge, but also to Sgurr a' Bhac Chaolais (885 m), the peak to the west of the bealach. There is a short 'mauvais pas' on the ridge between the bealach and Sgurr a' Bhac Chaolais which requires care when descending eastwards in winter conditions.

Sgurr na Sgine (945 m)

The next mountain to the west is Sgurr na Sgine. It is not well seen from Glen Shiel as it is hidden behind the very prominent conical peak of Faochag (c.900 m), which is linked to Sgurr na Sgine by a high crescent-shaped ridge enclosing the head of Coire Toteil. The east face of Sgurr na Sgine is about 250 m high and is very steep, a succession of scree gullies and ribs composed of grass and loose rock. A pleasant traverse of both peaks can be made by starting in Glen Shiel, following the Allt Mhalagain path to its crossing of the Allt Coire Toteil, and then continuing up the north side of this stream. There is no path, but the going is very easy. The direct ascent of the east side of Sgurr na Sgine is not recommended as the hazard in summer from falling rock is not inconsiderable. (In winter, under a good covering of frozen snow or ice, this face would probably give a very good climb). A better summer route, which still has a bit of rock to give it some interest, is the short north-east ridge whose foot is easily reached from the Allt Coire Toteil. An easier route lies further up the corrie, by an easy-angled grassy gully which leads to the ridge a short distance north of the summit, near the lower North-West Top (944 m). Approaching Sgurr na Sgine from the north, the summit is easily recognised even in the thickest of mist for the east face drops precipitously a few metres beyond the cairn. The traverse to Faochag is very pleasant, the ridge becoming quite narrow and very steep-sided, and the descent from Faochag to Glen Shiel can be made directly down its north-east ridge.

Sgurr na Sgine can also be climbed from Kinloch Hourn, although this route is rather neglected. The approach is by the right-of-way from Kinloch Hourn to Arnisdale, and there is a superb prospect down Loch Hourn from this route. A good circuit can be made by taking the right-of-way for 1½ km to its highest point above Loch Beag, and then climbing Buidhe Bheinn (879 m) by the stalker's path on its south-west side. Continue along the ridge to Sgurr a' Bhac Chaolais, traverse west to Sgurr na Sgine and descend its broad south-west ridge to reach a stalker's path which in turn leads to the right-of-way 2 km from Kinloch Hourn.

The Saddle (1010 m)

Two kilometres north-west of Sgurr na Sgine one comes to The Saddle, which is the culminating point of the great range of mountains on the south side of Glen Shiel. Although not quite the highest, it is certainly the finest of these mountains, and one of the finest in the Western Highlands. The summit is the meeting point of three ridges, and the plan of the mountain is rather like a letter E with the three prongs facing northwards. Between the prongs, or ridges, are two fine corries, the Coire Uaine to the west and the Coire Chaoil to the east, and the streams flowing from these corries unite to form the Allt Undalain which joins the River Shiel at Shiel Bridge.

The north ridge rises from the Allt Undalain, 3 km south of Shiel Bridge, and is steep and grassy at first with a band of rocks, then a narrower ridge to Sgurr na Creige and finally a more level section to the top. The west ridge starts a long way to the north-west of The Saddle, rises over Sgurr Leac nan Each (919 m) and Spidean Dhomhuill Bhric (940 m), and encloses the deep Coire Uaine whose headwall drops steeply to the west of the summit. The third ridge is the finest; this is the east ridge whose lower part overlooks Glen Shiel. The upper part, called the Forcan Ridge, is narrow and rocky for a few hundred metres as it rises to Sgurr na Forcan (960 m), dips and rises to the East Top (958 m) and finally reaches the summit. The summit of The Saddle is a level ridge about a 100 m long with a trig point at its west end and a cairn on top of the rocky buttress at the east end. The two points seem to be of equal height.

The best route of ascent of The Saddle is without any doubt the Forcan Ridge. Although it is narrow and rocky and some scrambling is involved if one stays right on the crest, there are no difficulties that cannot be avoided and the ascent of this ridge is unequalled in the Western Highlands. In winter, of course, the climb is likely to be much more serious, possibly even difficult. The climb starts in Glen Shiel, 1 km above Achnangart, and a good stalker's path leads up to the ridge between Biod an Fhithich and Meallan Odhar. The latter hill is traversed or contoured on its north-west side and the foot of the Forcan Ridge is reached. At first this ridge is easy, though rocky; then after a short drop it narrows almost to a knife edge and there is delightful scrambling right on the crest. On the left slabs fall sheer to Coire Mhalagain, but on the right the rocks are more broken and difficulties can be avoided on that side. All too soon the ridge ends at the top of Sgurr na Forcan. The traverse continues with a steep but easy pitch down to a gap in the ridge which continues, still quite narrow but easy, over the East Top and then steeply up to the cairn at the east end of the level summit ridge of The Saddle. This is one of the most pleasant climbs in all the Scottish mountains.

The descent should be made by a different route to complete a traverse of the mountain. The best option is to go west along the ridge to Spidean Dhomhuill Bhric and on to Sgurr Leac nan Each and north for a further 2 or 3 km before descending to the Allt Undalain. The quicker alternative is to descend the north ridge over Sgurr na Creige, avoiding the rock band lower down the ridge by a descent on the east side towards the Allt a' Choire Chaoil.

The traverse of The Saddle can quite easily be combined with Sgurr na Sgine, in which case the south-east ridge of Sgurr na Forcan above Bealach Coire Mhalagain will either have to be ascended or descended. This ridge is quite steep and rocky in its upper part, but should not present any difficulty.

Other starting points for the ascent of The Saddle are Kinloch Hourn and Arnisdale, but in both cases the approach to the mountain is fairly long. The right-of-way between these two points can be used to reach the ruined cottage in Gleann Dubh Lochain, from where a route can be made up the Mulloch Gorm ridge to Spidean Dhomhuill Bhric.

The most promising part of The Saddle for rock-climbing is the south

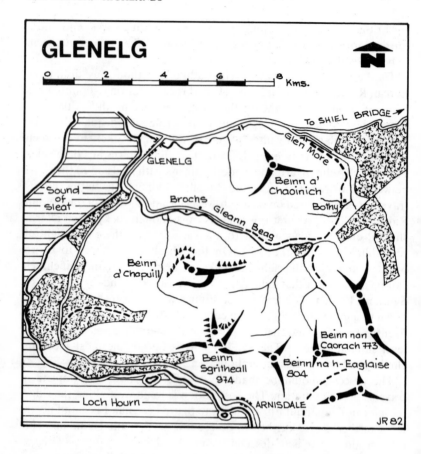

side of the Forcan Ridge. Approach by the route already described and diverge onto the south side of the ridge before it becomes steep and rocky, following a dry stone dyke which crosses the bouldery hillside towards the Bealach Coire Mhalagain. This brings one directly below slabby rocks on the flank of the Forcan Ridge. One route has been done by D. Niven, D. Sommerville and D. Bennet leading up to the bump on the Forcan Ridge which precedes the narrow rocky section (100 m, Difficult). Higher up in the corrie *Easter Buttress* is the fairly well defined buttress which leads to the upper part of the Forcan Ridge. It gives a good, clean, steep climb which is Severe if the crest is followed throughout. Easier climbing, about Very Difficult in standard, can be had by avoiding difficulties on the right. The climb finishes a few metres

45. *The view from Inverie across Loch Nevis towards Rum.*

46. *Luinne Bheinn from Meall Buidhe.*

47.   *The Rough Bounds of Knoydart: the view south-east from Ladhar Bheinn to Sgurr Mor (left), Luinne Bheinn and Sgurr na Ciche (right).*

48. *The north-west face of Stob a' Chearcaill rising above Coire na Cabaig.*

49. Ladhar Bheinn from Stob a' Chearcaill.

50. *Looking north from Coire Dhorrcail to Beinn Sgritheall across Loch Hourn.*

51.   Ladhar Bheinn from Barrisdale Bay.

52.   *The headwall of Coire Dhorrcail, with the summit of Ladhar Bheinn beyond.*

from the horizontal knife-edge just below the summit. (100 m, Severe) D. Piggott and G. S. Johnstone.

Coire Uaine should not be neglected for possible winter climbs, for it has a very steep headwall—too vegetatious to be of interest in summer, but worth a visit in good snow and ice conditions. The spur which drops steeply below the summit of Spidean Dhomhuill Bhric towards Loch a' Coire Uaine has been climbed in winter and is an interesting route.

Beinn Sgritheall (974 m)

The peninsula to the west of The Saddle has some very pleasant and varied scenery, particularly round the coast where there are many contrasting features: the forested hillsides above Loch Duich, the farmland around Glenelg and the steep mountains above Loch Hourn. The highest and finest mountain is Beinn Sgritheall which rises to the north of Arnisdale. Its south face rises directly from Loch Hourn in ever steepening slopes which high up become scree and broken rock buttresses which present a rather forbidding appearance; sufficient to deter anyone from a direct ascent of this face. The north side of the mountain has three remote corries; Coire Min, Coire Dubh and a third corrie, unnamed on the Ordnance Survey map, due north of the summit. The North-west Top (928 m) rises on the west side of this corrie.

The most straightforward ascent of Beinn Sgritheall starts from the roadside about 3 km north-west of Arnisdale, near the crag called Creag Ruadh. One climbs in a north-westerly direction up the beautiful wooded hillside of Coille Mhialairigh, looking for a path which leads to the ruins of a shieling among the trees. Above the shieling the path continues, very steeply in places, and eventually reaches the flat col about 2 km west of Beinn Sgritheall. The little lochan on this col may be a useful guide in thick weather. From there the ascent to the summit is straightforward, directly up the west ridge which is rocky in places. This is a very fine climb, with excellent views on a clear day beyond the mouth of Loch Hourn to Rum, and across the loch to the Knoydart mountains.

An alternative ascent from Arnisdale can be made directly behind the village, climbing steeply uphill towards the Bealach Arnasdail. It is probably best to keep on the east side of the stream which comes down from the bealach. From there one climbs a steep scree slope to reach the

H

east top of Beinn Sgritheall, followed by a delightful ridge walk to the summit.

The north side of the mountain is well worth exploration, but the approach is much longer than that from the south. Balvraid in Gleann Beag is the nearest starting point, and Suardalan bothy in Glen More is a good base for the exploration of the north side of Beinn Sgritheall and its neighbouring hills. The best ascent route is the Allt Srath a' Chomair and the north-east ridge of Beinn Sgritheall.

The north side of the North-west Top has given the only recorded rock climb on Beinn Sgritheall. The face above Loch Bealach na h-Oidhche is split by a big gully; to the left is a shallower gully, and further left is the North Buttress, consisting of three rock steps separated by grassy ledges. It has been climbed in both summer and winter conditions by H. M. Brown and companions. (130 m, Difficult).

Beinn na h-Eaglaise (804 m), Beinn nan Caorach (773 m)

The two hills to the east of Beinn Sgritheall, Beinn na h-Eaglaise and Beinn nan Caorach, are steep and in places scree-covered. Both can be climbed from Arnisdale in a single day, crossing the col at about 590 m between them.

Elsewhere in the peninsula there are some pleasant walks in Glen More, Gleann Beag and Glen Arnisdale, which will be described below. The two brochs in Gleann Beag, Dun Telve and Dun Trodden, are well worth a visit as the best preserved Pictish brochs on the Scottish mainland. At Glenelg there are the stark remains of the Bernera Barracks where a Hanoverian garrison was stationed in the eighteenth century. A third broch, Caisteal Grugaig, is situated in the forest 1 km west of Totaig at the northern tip of the peninsula overlooking Loch Alsh, but only a small part of the original walls remains.

Walks and Paths

Loch Quoich to Glen Shiel. Start at the road bridge over Loch Quoich's northern inlet, and take the private road to Alltbeithe. Then follow the right-of-way up Wester Glen Quoich to the Bealach Duibh Leac. On the north-west side of this pass the track is rather indistinct but it improves lower down and the last 2 km beside the Allt Mhalagain are good going (14 km).

Kinloch Hourn to Glen Shiel. Take the stalker's path from Kinloch Hourn or Loch Coire Shubh north-east up the Allt Coire Sgoireadail and cross the pass north-west of Sgurr a' Mhaoraich to descend into Glen Quoich, where the preceding route is joined. (This was the route taken by Prince Charles on his flight northwards in July 1746. When he reached Glen Shiel he hid near the cottage at Achnangart before continuing east to Glen Moriston). (10 km).

Kinloch Hourn to Arnisdale. This right-of-way goes steeply uphill behind Kinlochhourn House, climbing almost to 300 m behind a little knoll before descending slightly and continuing fiarly level to reach the head of Gleann Dubh Lochain. This glen is followed past its two lochans to the road between Arnisdale and Corran. The beauty of the first half of this walk has been spoiled by the large electricity transmission pylons which follow the path on their way to Skye (13 km).

Kinloch Hourn to Gleann Beag (or Glen More). Take the previous route to Gleann Dubh Lochain, but instead of turning south-west down this glen at the ruined cottage, continue north-west over the Bealach Aoidhdailean (hardly any trace of a path) and descend the glen on the far side to Srath a' Chomair, where a good track is joined. This track can either be followed west to Balvraid in Gleann Beag (17 km), or north-east past Suardalan bothy to Glen More (19 km).

Another variation of this walk can be made by going north from the ruined cottage in Gleann Dubh Lochain to the Bealach a' Chasain (c.580 m) (at map reference 911123), and descending into Glen More. One can either continue down this glen, or strike out eastwards by the Allt a' Ghleannain to cross another pass (c.470 m) and descend to the Allt Undalain and Shiel Bridge (20 km from Kinloch Hourn).

Finally, a pleasant coastal walk can be made from Totaig, past Ardintoul and along the shoreline of Loch Alsh and Kyle Rhea to Glenelg (13 km).

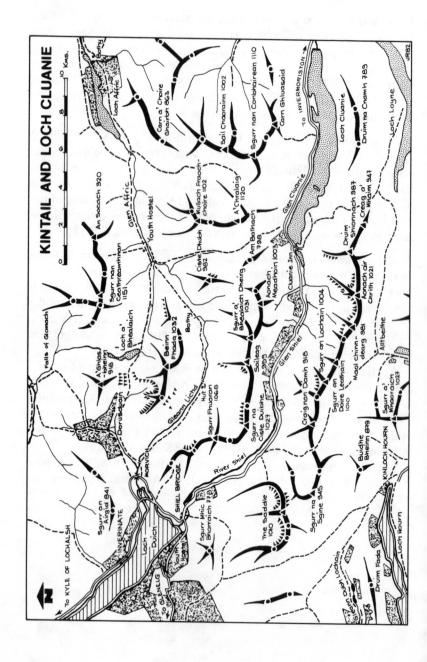

KINTAIL AND LOCH CLUANIE

Ciste Dhubh (982 m) 062166
Aonach Meadhoin (1003 m) 049138
Sgurr an Fhuarail (988 m) 054139
Sgurr a' Bhealaich Dheirg (1031 m) 034143
Saileag (959 m) 018148
Sgurr nan Spainteach (*c.*990 m) 992150
Sgurr na Ciste Duibhe (1027 m) 984149
Sgurr na Carnach (1002 m) 977159
Sgurr Fhuaran (1068 m) 978167
Sgurr nan Saighead (929 m) 975178
Sgurr na Moraich (876 m) 965193
Beinn Fhada (1032 m) 018193
A'Ghlas-bheinn (918 m) 008231
Sgurr an Airgid (841 m) 940227

Munro's Tables, Section 11

MAPS: Ordnance Survey 1:50,000 (2nd Series) Sheet 33.

The territory described in this chapter includes the Kintail and Inverinate forests, a compact area bounded on the south-west by Glen Shiel and Loch Duich, on the north by Loch Long and Glen Elchaig and on the east by Gleann Gaorsaic, Gleann Gniomhaidh to the point where it joins the River Affric near Alltbeithe, and from there due south through a deep glen to reach Loch Cluanie near its west end. This area is itself divided into two parts of quite different character by Strath Croe and its extension north-east over the Bealach na Sroine to the Falls of Glomach. To the east is Kintail, a very mountainous area best known for the superb range of mountains on the north-east side of Glen Shiel, the Five Sisters of Kintail. The Inverinate Forest to the north-west of Strath Croe is much less mountainous, there are no Munros and only one Corbett in this area, but it is nevertheless rugged country with a few rocky little hills and some fine crags which, being of Lewisian gneiss, are of more than passing interest to the rock-climber.

Much of Kintail, including the Five Sisters and some of the neighbouring mountains, is owned by the National Trust for Scotland, having been purchased by the Trust with funds given by Percy Unna, a past President of the Scottish Mountaineering Club. The normal restrictions which may apply to many of the West Highland mountains in the stalking season do not apply to the Kintail mountains which stand on Trust territory. The many and varied features of interest in Kintail and its surrounding country—splendid mountains such as the Five Sisters and The Saddle, the Falls of Glomach, Eilean Donnan Castle and the Pictish brochs near Glenelg to name a few—make it one of the most popular parts of the Western Highlands with climbers, walkers and tourists alike.

Access to the mountains to be described in this chapter is very easy, as the main road from the south to Kyle of Lochalsh and Skye (A87) passes close to most of them on its way through Glen Shiel. The bus services mentioned in the last chapter from Edinburgh, Glasgow and Inverness to Kyle of Lochalsh all pass through Glen Shiel and may be used as a way of getting to and from the mountains. There is a public road from Ardelve up the west side of Loch Long to the crofts at Camasluinie, but the road on the north side of the River Elchaig is private and closed to cars beyond Killilan unless permission is obtained to drive up the glen.

There are hotels at Cluanie, the head of Loch Duich and at Dornie and Ardelve on opposite sides of the mouth of Loch Long. Bed and breakfast houses abound, particularly at Ratagan and Inverinate where there are small communities of Forestry Commission workers, and there is also an abundance of caravans to let. The Scottish Youth Hostels Association has hostels at Ratagan by Loch Duich and Alltbeithe in remote Glen Affric, and there are camping and caravan sites at Shiel Bridge and Morvich in Strath Croe, the latter run by the National Trust for Scotland. In Gleann Lichd there is a climbers' hut at Glenlicht House leased by the Trust to the Edinburgh University Mountaineering Club, and near the watershed between Gleann Lichd and the Fionngleann (Glen Affric) the remote cottage at Camban has been renovated by the Mountain Bothies Association and is well placed in the heart of the mountains, a good shelter for climbers and walkers.

The fact that many of the Kintail mountains are on National Trust for Scotland territory and can be climbed at any season is fortunate, for many of the surrounding mountains are in stalking country, and there are quite likely to be restrictions on climbing them in late summer and autumn. The boundary of the National Trust for Scotland property is shown on the Ordnance Survey map.

The main mountains of Kintail are those on the north-east side of Glen Shiel—the Five Sisters and the ridge of four more mountains to the east which ends at Ciste Dhubh, 5 km north of Cluanie Inn. The entire range, from Ciste Dhubh to Sgurr na Moraich, the north-west outlier of the Five Sisters, is 15 km long and includes six Munros, and it might well be called the North Glen Shiel Ridge. By comparison with the South Glen Shiel Ridge it is a far finer range, the peaks are higher, steeper and have more individuality, the cols which separate them are lower and on the north side overlooking Gleann Lichd there are some magnificent corries with steep slabby buttresses and gullies. Although it is quite possible for fit climbers to traverse the whole ridge in a single day, this is a very strenuous expedition, much more so than the South Glen Shiel Ridge. Most climbers therefore take two days to climb all the peaks, one for the Five Sisters and a second day for the eastern half of the ridge. The col between the two halves, the Bealach an Lapain (723 m), is easily reached from Glen Shiel, and makes the fastest route up and down from the ridge.

Ciste Dhubh (982 m)

Ciste Dhubh, the easternmost of these mountains, is rather isolated from the others, its crest being a narrow ridge running from south to north, with the summit at the north end. An Caorann Mor is the deep glen to its east, and the Bealach a' Choinich (600 m) separates it from the next peaks to the south-west. The fine narrow ridge of Am Bathach (798 m) extends from the bealach towards Loch Cluanie, and it is really an extension of the Ciste Dhubh ridge. To the north of Ciste Dhubh steep slopes drop to the Fionngleann and Camban bothy, and the west side of the mountain is very steep indeed, dangerously so in conditions of soft snow. There are records of avalanche accidents on this mountain. The sharp-pointed summit of Ciste Dhubh can be glimpsed from the road near Loch Cluanie; it looks rather fine with the buttress just below it split by a prominent little gully. On closer inspection this summit buttress is found to be disappointing from the climbing point of view, being slabby rock and grass, but the gully has been climbed in winter conditions.

The normal route of ascent from Cluanie leads up the glen called An Caorann Beag. There are paths on both sides of the stream low down, but they soon disappear. Thereafter the going is quite easy up the grassy glen to the Bealach a' Choinich, and then steeply up the lower part of

Ciste Dhubh's south ridge to the narrow level crest which is followed very pleasantly to the summit. Am Bathach can be included in the ascent by traversing its ridge from Loch Cluanie to the Bealach a' Choinich. From the north Ciste Dhubh can be climbed directly from Camban by its north-north-west shoulder, or from Alltbeithe by its north-east shoulder.

Aonach Meadhoin (1003 m), Sgurr an Fhuarail (988 m)

To the south-west of the Bealach a' Choinich are the twin peaks of Aonach Meadhoin and Sgurr an Fhuarail, only the latter being named on the Ordnance Survey map. The main ridge runs roughly east to west over these two peaks and is quite narrow, giving them a fine appearance, but the traverse is perfectly easy. The ascent routes to Sgurr an Fhuarail are very straightforward, either the north-east ridge from the Bealach a' Choinich or the south-east ridge from Cluanie Inn, climbing over a small bump on the ridge at 800 m on the way.

Sgurr a' Bhealaich Dheirg (1031 m)

The east ridge of Aonach Meadhoin leads to the next mountain on the north side of Glen Shiel, Sgurr a' Bhealaich Dheirg. The summit ridge of this mountain is about 300 or 400 m long and fairly level; at its south-east end a subsidiary ridge goes out to the north-east. The summit is about a 100 m along this subsidiary ridge which is narrow and rocky, and a dry stone dyke leads to the splendidly built summit cairn which stands astride the ridge; one of the noblest cairns on any Scottish mountain. A short distance beyond the summit the ridge is cleft by a reddish gully to which the mountain may well owe its name.

If one is not traversing the North Glen Shiel Ridge, but simply looking for a quick route to Sgurr a' Bhealaich Dheirg, then the best starting point is near the Cluanie-Shiel watershed where a gap in the forest gives access to the Meall a' Charra ridge which in turn leads to the main ridge south-east of the mountain.

Saileag (959 m)

Going west from Sgurr a' Bhealaich Dheirg, the main ridge is quite narrow as it drops to the next col and rises to the grassy top of Saileag. This is not a very distinguished mountain; it has been described as a 'mere swelling in the ridge', but it does have a steep west face which looks impressive from the lower reaches of Gleann Lichd. One kilometre further west the broad grassy ridge drops to the Bealach an Lapain from which, as already mentioned, there is a steep, but fast and easy descent to Glen Shiel. There is also a descent route on the north side of the ridge down the Allt an Lapain to Gleann Lichd.

The Five Sisters of Kintail

The Five Sisters of Kintail are probably the best known mountains in the Western Highlands. Their appearance, particularly as seen from Loch Duich or the top of The Mam Ratagan, is very striking with the peaks showing their full height above sea-level and a remarkable symmetry of outline. The Five Sisters, from south-east to north-west are:—**Sgurr na Ciste Duibhe** (1027 m), **Sgurr na Carnach** (1002 m), **Sgurr Fhuaran** (1068 m), **Sgurr nan Saighead** (929 m) and **Sgurr na Moraich** (876 m).

Surprisingly, for the ridge which joins these peaks seems to go up and down a lot, there are only two Munros among the Five Sisters; the two highest. Another fine peak at the east end of the ridge which is not normally counted among the five (presumably as it is not seen from the lower part of Glen Shiel) is Sgurr nan Spainteach (c.990 m), the peak of the Spaniards. The name originates from the little known Battle of Glenshiel fought in 1719 when a small force of Jacobites supported by 300 Spanish soldiers who had landed on the west coast at Eilean Donnan castle was defeated by a Hanoverian army in Glen Shiel. In the heat of the battle the heather caught fire and the Spaniards had to retreat up the hillside, and some of them doubtless reached the peak which now bears their name.

On both its sides the ridge of the Five Sisters falls sheer into the glens below—Glen Shiel on the south-west and Gleann Lichd on the north-east. The south-west face of Sgurr na Ciste Duibhe falls 1000 m in a horizontal distance of $1\frac{1}{4}$ km, one of the longest and steepest continuous slopes in Scotland. Lower down Glen Shiel the Five Sisters are characterised by the long grassy spurs of Sgurr Fhuaran and Sgurr na Carnach, separated by deep gullies. The Gleann Lichd side is much wilder, and there are some superb corries on this remote side of the ridge. The few winter climbs recorded in these corries have been done by members of the Edinburgh University Mountaineering Club, based at their hut at Glenlicht House.

The classic expedition is of course the traverse of the Five Sisters, and it should be done from east to west for two reasons, firstly the best views are ahead, and secondly the ascent to the ridge at the Bealach an Lapain is far easier than the climb to the north-west end of the ridge from Loch Duich or the lower part of Glen Shiel. The start of the traverse is very obvious, at the gap in the forest almost 2 km east of the site of the Battle of Glenshiel. The ascent is steep and unrelenting up a grassy slope, but there is a faint path worn by climbers for most of the way, and an hour should suffice to reach the bealach. The narrow grassy ridge rises gradually westwards to Sgurr nan Spainteach, and then drops more abruptly, with a rocky pitch down to the col below Sgurr na Ciste Duibhe. At this col there is a curious hollow in the crest of the ridge, which one passes either to the left or the right before climbing steeply to the big cairn of Sgurr na Ciste Duibhe. (This feature can be very confusing in thick mist, particularly if one is going from west to east). The main ridge now swings round northwards and is broad and bouldery over Sgurr na Carnach and down to the col below Sgurr Fhuaran, whose ascent is steep for 200 m.

From Sgurr Fhuaran descend west-north-west for a short distance before turning right off this ridge (which continues down to Glen Shiel) and traversing downwards on a path which rejoins the main ridge below the rather steep summit slopes of the peak. The ridge to Sgurr nan Saighead gives a good view of the steep slabby east face of that peak, which appears very much as a pyramid from this point of view. One also gets a good impression of the typical rock structure of the Kintail mountains, flaggy granulites and mica-schists set at a steep angle, presenting smooth slabby faces with a lot of vegetation, and gullies filled with scree and loose rock. It is not surprising that most of the climbing on the crags of the Five Sisters has been done in winter.

Beyond the highest point of Sgurr nan Saighead the ridge drops again, becoming very narrow indeed for a short distance to the lower north-west peak. This point commands a very fine view, both in a south-easterly direction towards the peaks of the Five Sisters, and also in the opposite direction down Loch Duich to Skye. The last of the Five Sisters, Sgurr na Moraich, has a long broad summit ridge and a continuously steep descent to Ault a' Chruinn at the head of Loch Duich.

Alternative descents from the north-west peak of Sgurr nan Saighead are firstly down the Allt a' Chruinn where a path is joined low down just above the rocky gorge and waterfall, which are traversed on the east side, and secondly down the grassy north-west ridge to the col below Sgurr an t-Searraich followed by a steep descent south-west to cross the River Shiel by the footbridge just above Loch Shiel. Either of these two routes can be used for the ascent of the north-west end of the Five Sisters ridge, and if one's objective is Sgurr Fhuaran alone, then the best ascent route is its west-north-west ridge, one of the longest continuous climbs in Scotland and a well-known grind, for one has to climb from glen to summit without any respite. (Note that the bridge marked on the Ordnance Survey map over the River Shiel opposite Torrlaoighseach does not exist).

It is likely that many winter climbs have been done in the Gleann Lichd corries of the Five Sisters, but most of them have gone unrecorded. The following four routes for which descriptions do exist give some idea of the possibilities of these mountains in winter. The access to these climbs is long, unless one happens to be staying in the climbers' hut at Glenlicht House. (S.M.C.J., Vol. XXVI, No. 148, p. 155 for these climbs).

On Sgurr nan Spainteach *Solo Gully* is an obvious line on the left side of the corrie between this peak and Sgurr na Ciste Duibhe. Climbed in crampons, it was found to be straightforward with two very short ice pitches and it finished on the ridge 200 m east of the summit of Sgurr nan Spainteach (120 m, Grade II) J. G. Burns.

The east face of Sgurr na Carnach is very steep and broken, and has one prominent gully, *Dog's Leg Gully*, which starts near the foot of the face and forks half way up. The left fork leads over a rocky bluff (well iced on the first ascent) and finishes within a few metres of the summit (180 m, Grade II) J. H. Barber and J. G. Burns.

The north face of Sgurr Fhuaran has a steep dark crag immediately below the summit. An obvious gully splits this crag from top to bottom, with a triple fork in its upper reaches. On the first ascent the centre fork was climbed, there being three short steep ice pitches and a vertical exit near the summit (220 m, Grade II/III) J. G. Burns and H. Kindness.

The north face of Sgurr nan Saighead, which is well seen from the north-west top, is composed of several buttresses divided by deep, narrow gullies. *Forked Gully* is the prominent gully in the centre of the face with a wide scree cone beneath it. On the first ascent the left hand fork was climbed, giving a steep climb finishing with a short ice pitch. J. H. Barber and C. A. Simpson.

One summer rock climb has been recorded on the east face of Sgurr nan Saighead. The climb, *California*, is up an obvious S-shaped crack at the apex of the left hand of two large scree cones. The chimney was climbed for about 8 m, and the right wall for 13 m. A further 16 m of loose stones led to a belay. A much narrower chimney, a short wall (crux) and another 20 m of climbing led to a belay, beyond which scrambling led to easy ground (80 m, Severe) J. H. Barber and C. A. Simpson.

Beinn Fhada (1032 m)

To the north of the Five Sisters is Beinn Fhada. Its name, meaning the long mountain, is very appropriate for it stretches for 8 km from the head of Loch Duich to Glen Affric. It has very steep slopes dropping on the south-west side into Gleann Lichd, so steep that there are no reasonable routes of ascent from this glen. On the north-east side there are several fine corries with intervening ridges. Unlike the Five Sisters, Beinn Fhada does not show its grandeur to every traveller on the road to Skye; its summit is far withdrawn behind outlying tops. From the road causeway at the head of Loch Duich the western peak, Sgurr a' Choire Ghairbh (c.870 m) appears as a fairly level ridge with several rounded knolls, the Faradh Nighean Fhearchair. These knolls are the crests of a series of steep slabby buttresses dropping on the other side of the ridge into Choire Chaoil, the finest of Beinn Fhada's corries. The crest of the ridge drops southwards to a prominent col, the Bealach an t-Sealgaire, the Hunters' Pass, and rises to the next peak, Ceum na h-Aon-choise (c.910 m), and continues quite level and narrow to Meall an Fhuarain Mhoir (956 m). Near this peak a spur juts out northwards separating Coire Gorm (as the upper part of Choire Chaoil is called) from Coire an Sgairne to the east. This corrie is ringed by crags, but they are too broken to be of climbing interest.

Thus far the mountain and its summit ridge are very fine; the drop on the Gleann Lichd side is spectacularly steep. Continuing east however, the character of the mountain changes completely and the next 2 km to the summit are across a wide featureless plateau, the Plaide Mhor. Beyond the summit the main crest of the mountain continues south at first and then east, circling round the big Coire an t-Siosalaich to reach Sgurr a' Dubh Doire (963 m), the sharp-pointed eastern peak which is prominent in views up Glen Affric. Beyond this peak the main ridge of Beinn Fhada drops gently in a further 4 km to the River Affric near Alltbeithe. One other feature of the mountain deserves mention; about 1 km north-west of the summit a broad ridge runs out northwards on the east side of Coire an Sgairne ending at Meall a' Bhealaich, from which the drop north to the Bealach an Sgairne is very steep and rocky.

The normal starting point for the ascent of Beinn Fhada is at Morvich in Strath Croe. Two very fine routes are possible, and the following combination of them is recommended as an excellent traverse of the mountain. From the cottage at Innis a' Chrotha climb easy grass slopes to Beinn Bhuidhe and continue up this broad grassy spur aiming for a knoll at the north end of the Sgurr a' Choire Ghairbh ridge. From this knoll descend a short distance to a col (which can be reached directly) and continue to Sgurr a' Choire Ghairbh. (There is a cairn about 100 m north-north-west of the top, which itself has only a tiny cairn). Continue south along the undulating ridge to the Hunters' Pass where there is a steep descent of 25 m which calls for a little care, but is not difficult. The ridge continues to Meall an Fhuarain Mhoir, and the final 2 km to the summit are across the Plaide Mhor, dropping slightly at first and them climbing a very gentle slope to the large cairn. The Plaide Mhor is rather an anticlimax to a very interesting climb, but if visibility is bad it will give some good navigation practice. Descend west and then north-west along the ridge leading to Meall a' Bhealaich and near its lowest point (at map reference 010206) join the stalker's path which zig-zags down into Coire an Sgairne to meet the path in Gleann Choinneachain, which in turn is followed back to Morvich.

From the east Beinn Fhada can be climbed easily over Sgurr a' Dubh Doire from the youth hostel at Alltbeithe or from the bothy at Camban. A traverse along the whole mountain combining this route with one of the two described in the preceding paragraph is a very fine expedition.

Climbs on Beinn Fhada are concentrated on the east face of Sgurr a' Choire Ghairbh, where a series of slabby buttresses overlooks the Choire Chaoil. The appearance of these buttresses is quite attractive from a distance, but on closer acquaintance a great deal of grass and other vegetation is apparent. N. Tennent described them aptly as appearing to be 'all rock when seen from below, and all grass when seen from above'. It may well be that the best climbing will be found in winter in conditions of well frozen snow and grass.

Under the summit of Sgurr a' Choire Ghairbh there is a broad buttress split into three parts by two narrow gullies. Two routes have been done:—

Summit Buttress (160 m, Difficult) D. Piggott and G. S. Johnstone. Start to the right of the right-hand gully and climb grassy slabs to a

113

prominent bulge about mid-height. Traverse left across the right-hand gully to the central part of Summit Buttress and climb this direct to the top on better rock. One avoidable Severe pitch was climbed.

Right-Hand Gully (160 m, Grade II/III) C. L. Donaldson, J. Russell and G. Dutton. On the first ascent the climb was found to be mainly on snow, with two pitches of considerable difficulty. (S.M.C.J., Vol. XXV, No. 143, p. 70).

To the left of *Summit Buttress* is a broad grassy gully enclosed by steep walls. The left wall forms the edge of *Needle's Eye Buttress*, so called after a square projection half way up the buttress which is pierced by a hole. (150 m, Difficult) R. Grieve and and R. Brown. The line of the climb is up the crest of the buttress, which becomes very narrow towards the top. The original account mentioned several pitches, but N. Tennent found the climb to be indeterminate, with a good deal of vegetation. (S.M.C.J., Vol. XXIV, No. 141, p. 235).

To the left of *Needle's Eye Buttress* is another broad grassy gully with a broad buttress to its left. The right hand edge of this buttress is formed, in its upper half, by a steep narrow rib, described as follows:—
Guides' Rib (100 m, Very Difficult) G. H. Kitchen and R. J. Porter. The rib is climbed in pitches of 15, 15 and 25 m to a large block. A short groove on the right leads to the top of the block. The rib continues for 12 m to a level arête leading to a narrow wall which is climbed to a little pinnacle above which the rib leads to easy ground. (S.M.C.J., Vol. XXVI, No. 147, p. 50).

To the left of *Guide's Rib*, and starting at the lowest point of the same buttress, is *Porter's Climb* (130 m, Difficult) G. H. Kitchen and R. J. Porter. From a cairn at the left edge of the lowest section of the buttress the climb goes in pitches of 22, 27 and 15 m near the left edge of vegetatious slabs to the base of steeper rock. Climb this on the right to the foot of a crack, followed to a large rocky stance. Easy slabs, a corner on the left and grassy groove (or difficult slab) lead to the top of a small pinnacle and easy ground. Twenty metres to the right of the finish of this climb, and at the same level, is a grass ledge below a steep wall. This wall and the slab above were climbed by the same party, and named *Continuation Climb* (30 m, Difficult). (S.M.C.J., Vol. XXVI, No. 147, p. 50).

A few hundred metres further left, towards the Hunters' Pass, there is a slabby buttress culminating in a fine pinnacle. The one route on this buttress is *The Needle* (110 m, Severe) J. R. Marshall, W. J. Cole and I. Oliver. The route goes up the north edge of the buttress. Starting from the lowest point climb the groove to the edge of the slab. Traverse right to a rib of porphyry (spike belay); the direct ascent of the slab is Severe. Excellent climbing leads up the rib in pitches of 10, 30 and 20 m to a cairn. Traverse to the right for 10 m to a large vibrating flake. Climb the wall above for 10 m to the top of a pinnacle (a magnificent situation), cross a narrow gap and scramble up to the top. (S.M.C.J., Vol. XXV, No. 144, p. 153).

A short distance further up the corrie, beyond the Hunters' Pass, the north-east buttress of Ceum na h-Aon-choise has been climbed in semi-winter conditions by N. Tennent and party, and is described as steep and loose; evidently a route better suited to hard winter conditions.

A'Ghlas-bheinn (918 m)

This little mountain lies to the north of Beinn Fhada, and is separated from it by the Bealach an Sgairne. It is in the Inverinate estate, and is not a very distinguished mountain, being rather knobbly in appearance. It is most easily climbed by taking the path from Dorusduain in Strath Croe towards the Bealach na Sroine and, once out of the forest, climbing directly up the west ridge of the mountain. Another route is via the Bealach an Sgairne, and the ascent of A'Ghlas-bheinn can be combined with Beinn Fhada in which case, if one is descending from Beinn Fhada, it is necessary to be very careful on the descent to the Bealach an Sgairne. The north side of Meall a' Bhealaich is steep and rocky, and the best line of descent is probably to the east of the deep gully which cuts this face. The ascent to A'Ghlas-bheinn from the bealach has a few rock outcrops, but is perfectly easy.

The ascent of A'Ghlas-bheinn can also be very easily combined with a visit to the Falls of Glomach, in which case the north ridge of the mountain will either have to be climbed or descended over a couple of knolls and past two little lochans. The west side of this ridge overlooking the Bealach na Sroine has some fair sized crags, and any descent of this hillside should be undertaken with care.

Sgurr an Airgid (841 m)

To the west of Strath Croe and the Bealach na Sroine one is in the Inverinate Forest. The highest hill in this area is Sgurr an Airgid on the north side of the head of Loch Duich. This hill has the reputation of being a very fine viewpoint, so the ascent is best kept for a good day. It takes only a couple of hours to climb up the stalker's path from Ruarach in Strath Croe to the col east of Sgurr an Airgid, and then $1\frac{1}{2}$ km along the ridge to the top.

Further west, beyond Coire Dhuinnid, the landscape changes and there are several little rocky hills rising from the undulating moorland. One of the most prominent of these is Boc Beag (c.420 m). It has a remarkably steep rocky summit, reminiscent of Ben A'n in the Trossachs, and as the rock is Lewisian gneiss, it is worth a visit for its rock-climbing possibilities. Leaving the Carr Brae road at its highest point, one climbs uphill to a sheepfold and then eastwards following a sheep track to reach the foot of the hill. There are two tiers of rock, the upper one being well seen from the approach, but the lower one is hidden and one has to descend eastwards a short distance to its foot. The most obvious feature of this lower tier is a smooth slab 30 m high, the *Leac Beag* (the little slab). The rock is excellent. Several climbs have been done on both tiers by N. Tennent and various companions, all about 25 to 30 m long and about Very Difficult in standard. Wisely, Tennent neither graded nor named these routes, leaving others to follow and enjoy the same sense of discovery. The author will do likewise, saying only that climbing on this little hill is great fun and the views towards the Cuillin are unsurpassed.

Another crag of a more serious nature in the Inverinate Forest is Biod an Fhithich, a fine west facing buttress 2 km east of Bundalloch on the east side of Loch Long. The approach is along the path on the south side of the River Glennan with a steep climb up grass to the foot of the buttress. Features of Biod an Fhithich are the very steep, in places overhanging, left hand side of the cliff which is rather vegetatious, the clean slabby right hand half, and the easy-angled ridge which bounds it on the right. Immediately to the right of this ridge is a narrow grassy gully, and beyond it a smaller vegetatious crag. A grassy rake rises rightwards below the crag and gives access to the foot of the steep wall below the slabs.

The first ascent of Biod an Fhithich was made by N. Tennent in 1961, and has been repeated by other parties. (See S.M.C.J., Vol. XXX, p. 271). All routes are on the slabby right hand half of the buttress. Tennent's route starts near the left hand edge of these slabs, up a vertical pitch with excellent holds. Higher up the climb is open to some variation and there is no single well-defined route, but the general

53. Loch Hourn from the north-east ridge of Ladhar Bheinn above Barrisdale Bay.

54. Looking across Loch Loyne to Spidean Mialach and Gleouraich (left) and the South Glen Shiel Ridge.

55.   Spidean Mialach (left) and Gleouraich (right) from Creag nan Damh.

56. *The South Glen Shiel Ridge: approaching Sgurr an Lochain from the south-east.*

57.   *Looking towards The Saddle from Sgurr na Forcan.*

58.   *The Forcan Ridge of The Saddle.*

59.   Faochag (left) and The Saddle from Glen Shiel.

60. *Looking east from The Saddle towards Sgurr a' Bhealaich Dheirg.*

61.   *A pinnacle on the Forcan Ridge of The Saddle.*

character of the climbing is slabby, with several heather ledges and a scarcity of belays. (120 m, Very Difficult). The right hand bounding ridge of the buttress is a succession of rock pitches separated by grass ledges, with considerable scope for variation (130 m, Difficult).

Walks and Paths

The cross-country route from Strath Glass to Kintail by Glen Affric will be described in the next chapter.

Cluanie Inn to Loch Duich. Two variations are possible, both take the track which starts $1\frac{1}{2}$ km east of Cluanie as a rough road up An Caorann Mor. This road becomes a path across the watershed and down to Glen Affric 1 km upstream from Alltbeithe youth hostel. The bridge over the river is opposite the hostel, but only if the river is in spate will it be necessary to make the long diversion eastwards to cross the bridge. One variation of the route now goes up the Fionngleann, following the path past Camban bothy and over the pass to Gleann Lichd. The scenery in this glen is very fine, particularly in the gorge of the Allt Grannda where the path crosses a very steep hillside as it drops towards Glenlicht House, beyond which a track leads to Morvich (23 km).

The alternative route after reaching Glen Affric is to go up Gleann Gniomhaidh by a good path, crossing the pass at its head and descending very slightly to go round the head of Loch a' Bhealaich. The path climbs again to the narrow defile of the Bealach an Sgairne, a fine pass, and then drops down Gleann Choinneachain to Strath Croe where one can either cross the river to Dorusduain or stay on its south side to reach Morvich (22 km).

The circuit of Beinn Fhada, starting and finishing at Morvich, is a very fine walk indeed. It is just a combination of the Gleann Lichd and the Gleann Gniomhaidh–Bealach an Sgairne sections of the routes described in the last paragraphs (26 km).

Glen Elchaig to Strath Croe by the Falls of Glomach. This route can be used as an approach to the Falls of Glomach either from Glen Elchaig or from Strath Croe. As already mentioned, the road up Glen Elchaig is private beyond Killilan and cars are not permitted. However, it may be possible to obtain permission to drive up the glen as far as the south-west end of Loch na Leitreach where there is a small car parking place at the start of the path to the Falls. One should telephone the owner of the Killilan Estate, Mrs Douglas, Killilan 272.

From the parking place the footpath, recently repaired, crosses the River Elchaig by the A. E. Robertson Memorial Bridge, and a short distance further crosses the Allt a' Ghlomaich by another footbridge. Then the path climbs into the steep and narrow ravine of the Allt a' Ghlomaich, traversing along the precipitous hillside, crossing the Allt na Laoidhre and climbing higher still to traverse high above the stupendous chasm of the Glomach. Eventually the path reaches a point above the Falls and one has to descend steeply and carefully to reach a superb balcony facing directly into the chasm down which the waters of the Allt a' Ghlomaich plunge in two great leaps. There is another and distinctly more exciting approach to the Falls. After crossing the Allt na Laoidhre one climbs a short distance uphill to a grassy knoll from which there is a glimpse of the Falls, and at this point a lower path crosses the steep side of the gorge. It is very narrow and exposed, and at one or two points one has to cross some rocks which are often wet. On reaching the end of this path one has to climb up a short easy pitch to reach the balcony referred to above. This is a superb approach to the Falls, the gorge having the character of a Himalayan valley, albeit on a small scale; those with a bad head for heights will, however, probably find it a bit too exciting, and it is best left for a dry day, being potentially quite hazardous in wet conditions. Having inspected the Falls, one climbs back to the high level path which turns to the south-west and climbs over the Bealach na Sroine before descending to the forest above Dorusduain and the public road in Strath Croe (8 km from the car park in Glen Elchaig to the car park in Strath Croe).

10

Strath Cluanie and Glen Affric

Carn Ghluasaid (957 m) 146125
Sgurr nan Conbhairean (1109 m) 130139
Sail Chaorainn (1002 m) 133155
A'Chralaig (1120 m) 094148
Mullach Fraoch-choire (1102 m) 095172
Toll Creagach (1053 m) 194283
Tom a' Choinich (1111 m) 163273
Carn Eige (1183 m) 123262
Mam Sodhail (1181 m) 120253
Beinn Fhionnlaidh (1005 m) 115283
An Socach (920 m) 088230
Sgurr nan Ceathreamhnan (1151 m) 057229
Mullach na Dheiragain (982 m) 081259

Munro's Tables, Section 11

MAPS: Ordnance Survey 1:50,000 (2nd Series) Sheets 25, 26, 33, 34.

To the east and north-east of Kintail the Western Highland landscape takes on a larger and more spacious scale. The mountains are higher and more massive, and the glens and straths longer, wider and in places magnificently wooded. The appearance of the country is very different from Knoydart or Morar, less rough and rugged maybe, but having a grandeur that fully compensates, and gives these mountains and glens something of the character of the Cairngorms. The mountains have much smoother contours than the rough and sharp peaks of Knoydart and Kintail, and they are characterised by long ridges enclosing many fine corries, but few of these corries have much in the way of steep cliffs and crags, rather they are great bowls carved by ancient glaciers out of the mountainsides. The difference in appearance between these mountains and their lower southern neighbours is probably that,

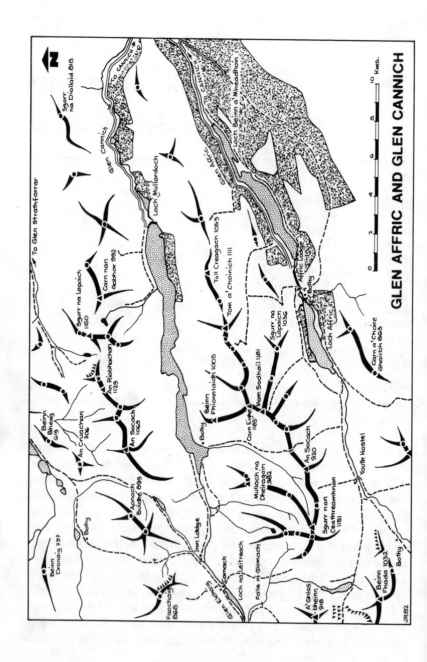

GLEN AFFRIC AND GLEN CANNICH

because of their central position in the Highlands, an ice cap could have existed to protect them from the effects of valley glaciation in the Ice Age.

The area to be described in this chapter is bounded on the south side by Glen Moriston and Strath Cluanie, on the north by Glen Urquhart and Glen Cannich, on the east by Loch Ness and the western boundary is Gleann Gaorsaic, Gleann Gniomhaidh and An Caorann Mor. Glen Affric is in the heart of this area. It is one of the finest of all Scottish glens, and between its highest reaches and the Beauly Firth where its waters reach the sea there is a richness and variety of scenery that few glens can match. The headwaters of the River Affric rise high in the corries of the Kintail mountains, close under the summits of Beinn Fhada and Sgurr a' Bhealaich Dheirg, and flow down to the great confluence of streams and glens near Alltbeithe, the remotest of Scottish youth hostels. For the next 7 km the river meanders between grassy flats, and several ruined cottages testify that once this part of the glen was inhabited and cattle grazed along the banks of the river. Now only the cottage at Athnamulloch is occupied by a shepherd in summer. At Loch Affric the forests begin; on the north side are the remnants of the Old Caledonian Forest, and on the south side these fine old pine trees are now mixed with the more densely planted conifers of the Forestry Commission. At the east end of Loch Affric, in a splendid position on a wooded knoll, stands Affric Lodge, and 2 km further east one comes to Loch Beinn a' Mheadhoin (pronounced Loch Benevain). This is the part of Glen Affric much seen and admired by car-borne tourists, for the public road goes as far as the head of this loch. From there down to Fasnakyle, where the River Affric enters Strath Glass, there is one of the most beautiful stretches of woodland in the Highlands, birch and pine, through which the river carves its turbulent way. In fact the River Affric is distinctly less turbulent nowadays since the North of Scotland Hydro-Electric Board built a dam across the east end of Loch Beinn a' Mheadhoin, and most of the waters of Affric and Cannich now flow down to Fasnakyle through underground pipes. At the village of Cannich one is in Strath Glass, and this valley extends for almost 30 km to the Beauly Firth, presenting a wonderfully varied landscape of cultivated land, forests and hills.

The other glens in the area of this chapter also have their own distinctive features. Glen Cannich is often spoken of as the twin of Glen Affric, but the similarity between the two is not great. Like Affric, Cannich is finely wooded in its lower reaches as far west as the huge

121

dam which impounds Loch Mullardoch. This greatly enlarged loch, whose waters flow south to keep Loch Beinn a' Mheadhoin topped up, extends for 13 km almost to the head of the glen, which is barren and treeless except for some fine old pines on the south side of the loch. Changes in the level of Loch Mullardoch create a rather ugly 'tide-mark' along its entire length, and at the head of the loch when the water level is low there is an extensive muddy area of no great beauty. Nevertheless, despite these features, there is an undeniable grandeur about Glen Cannich, surrounded as it is by the five highest mountains of the Western Highlands.

Glen Urquhart and lower Glen Moriston are hardly mountain glens, but they are both beautifully wooded and between them there is a vast tract of rough undulating moorland dotted with innumerable lochs and lochans; not climbing country, but a fisherman's paradise. The most prominent feature of this area is the distinctive rounded dome of Meall Fuar-mhonaidh (696 m) which rises steeply above Loch Ness between Invermoriston and Drumnadrochit. It has the distinction of being the highest Old Red Sandstone mountain in the country. The upper part of Glen Moriston, extending to Strath Cluanie with its enlarged Loch Cluanie, has some of the same character as Glen Cannich, but it carries the main road to Skye and thus lacks the wilderness character of Cannich.

The mountains described in this chapter can all be climbed from Glen Affric, with a lot of walking in some cases. They can conveniently be divided into two groups. To the south there is a group of five Munros between Loch Affric and Loch Cluanie which can be most easily climbed from Cluanie-side. To the north, forming the watershed between Glen Affric and Glen Cannich, there is a long range of mountains with eight Munros, several Tops and many subsidiary ridges which in its height and scale is the grandest of the many long east-west chains of mountains in the Western Highlands.

Access to the mountains can be made from at least three directions. In the south the A87 road passes through upper Glen Moriston and Strath Cluanie. In the west the closest access is either from Dorusduain in Strath Croe, or (if one has permission to drive up Glen Elchaig) from the car park near Loch na Leitreach. The main route of access, however, is up Glen Affric where the public road goes to the west end of Loch Beinn a' Mheadhoin. From there the right-of-way to Kintail continues on the north side of Loch Affric, and there is a Forestry Commission road for several kilometres up the south side of the glen. Buses from

Inverness, Edinburgh and Glasgow to Kyle of Lochalsh pass through Strath Cluanie, there is a bus service from Inverness to Cannich via Glen Urquhart and a Post Bus service from Beauly to Cannich via Strath Glass.

There are hotels at Cannich and Struy in Strath Glass, Invermoriston and Drumnadrochit (both rather far from the mountains), Cluanie and Loch Duich. Bed and breakfasts and caravans to let abound, particularly in Cannich, Strath Glass, Glen Urquhart and Kintail. Accommodation is (at the time of writing) available at Cozac Lodge at the east end of Loch Mullardoch. There are three youth hostels of interest: Cannich, Ratagan and Alltbeithe. The last named, situated high up in Glen Affric at the very heart of the mountains, is the best base for hill-walking in the area described in this chapter. Although officially open only in the summer months, the hostel is unlocked during the rest of the year. However, it goes without saying that anyone using the hostel at such times is under an obligation to respect this facility and cause no damage whatsoever.

There are bothies at Loch Affric owned by the Forestry Commission, at map reference 181225, and at Camban 3 km up the Fionngleann from Alltbeithe. Near the west end of Loch Mullardoch there is a tiny wood and corrugated iron hut which in 1980 gave the author good shelter once some roof repairs were done, but such was the state of the hut that it may well have blown away by the time this book is in print. If it survives, however, it is a very useful base from which to climb the most inaccessible of the mountains described in this chapter and the next.

Like many of the districts of the Western Highlands, Glen Moriston and Glen Affric have their associations with Prince Charles during his flight after Culloden. His travels took him north from Morar to Glen Shiel where he stayed at Achnangart before moving east through Strath Cluanie and over Sgurr nan Conbhairean to a hiding place in Coire Mheadhoin on the north-east side of that mountain. This spot, known as Prince Charlie's Cave, is marked on the present edition of the Ordnance Survey map and is worth a visit despite its inaccessibility. It resembles the Shelter Stone in the Cairngorms, being formed from several large fallen boulders. After a week in this hiding place the Prince moved north with his bodyguard to Athnamulloch in Glen Affric, then down the glen to Fasnakyle and north over the hills to Glen Cannich. This was the Prince's furthest north point before he turned south and returned to Loch Arkaig by Glen Moriston and Tomdoun.

Carn Ghluasaid (957 m), Sgurr nan Conbhairean (1109 m), Sail Chaorainn (1002 m)

The southern group of mountains, those between Strath Cluanie and Glen Affric, is divided into two halves by Gleann na Ciche and the Bealach Choire a' Chait. The eastern part consists of Carn Ghluasaid, Sgurr nan Conbhairean and Sail Chaorainn. These three mountains form a crescent-shaped ridge whose northern outpost is Tigh Mor na Seilge (929 m), a Top of Sail Chaorainn. The east side of this 5 km ridge is a series of fine wild corries in which rise the headwaters of the River Doe, a tributary of the Moriston. It is high in one of these corries, under the crags of Sail Chaorainn, that the Prince's Cave is to be found. The west side of the ridge is a more uniform grassy slope dropping steeply to Gleann na Ciche.

These three mountains can be easily climbed in a single day from the side of Loch Cluanie. Starting at Lundie (where there is nothing more than the foundations of an old cottage by the lochside) one follows the old military road, now no more than a footpath, west to the junction with a stalker's path which leads up the south side of Carn Ghluasaid. This path gives an easy climb right up the flat summit plateau, and ends a few hundred metres south-west of the summit itself. In bad visibility it may be difficult to find the rather small cairn which marks the summit, so one should cross the plateau to its abrupt northern edge where there is a cairn from which the summit is about 50 m southwards. On a clear day the view from Carn Ghluasaid to Sgurr nan Conbhairean is very fine for there are some grand corries between the two peaks. The ridge north-westwards to Sgurr nan Conbhairean is very easy over the flat top of Creag a' Chaorainn (999 m) and across the Glas Bhealach; in places the grass is as smooth and close cropped as a golf course. The summit of Sgurr nan Conbhairean is crowned by a fine cairn with a little sheltered niche on its east side looking down to Coire Dho.

The traverse north to Sail Chaorainn is also very easy and one can continue north along a hummocky ridge to Carn na Coire Mheadhoin (1001 m) and Tigh Mor na Seilge, whose summit ridge is very narrow for a short distance with an impressive drop on the south side into Coire Mheadhoin. The return south should be by the same route at least as far as the top of Sgurr nan Conbhairean; from there a different way can be taken for the descent by going south-west to the col above the Gorm Lochan and up to the little top of Drochaid an Tuill Easaich (1000 m). From there the ridge southwards is easy going and at its foot one can head south-east to regain the old military road and follow it back to the day's starting point.

A'Chralaig (1120 m), Mullach Fraoch-choire (1102 m)

A'Chralaig and Mullach Fraoch-choire form a fine high ridge 8 km long running from south to north between Loch Cluanie and Glen Affric. The east side of this ridge drops to the Allt na Ciche, a tributary of the River Affric, in a series of large grassy corries, and the west side drops steeply to the deep glen between Cluanie and Alltbeithe, the Allt a' Chomhlain and An Caorann Mor.

A'Chralaig is normally climbed from Loch Cluanie, leaving the road near the foot of An Caorann Mor and climbing the steep grassy hillside north-eastwards to reach the south ridge at about 700 m where it becomes quite narrow and well-defined. Higher up the ridge is level for a short distance and a subsidiary ridge goes out north-east for $1\frac{1}{2}$ km to A'Chioch (948 m). The summit of A'Chralaig is crowned by a huge cairn, visible for miles around. The north ridge leads in $1\frac{1}{2}$ km to Stob Coire na Cralaig (1008 m) and the ridge then turns north-east and drops to its lowest point before rising to Mullach Fraoch-choire, the last $\frac{1}{2}$ km being a narrow ridge over a succession of pinnacles which are not difficult to traverse. On the north side of Mullach Fraoch-choire two ridges lead out towards Glen Affric, one to the north-west and the other north-eastwards over a small top, enclosing the Fraoch-choire, the heathery corrie, between them. The north-west ridge is the best route of ascent if one is coming from Alltbeithe, and the north-east ridge if one has walked up Glen Affric past Athnamulloch into Gleann na Ciche.

A very fine circuit of this group can be made from Glen Affric, climbing Mullach Fraoch-choire, traversing to A'Chralaig and descending its south-east ridge for just over $\frac{1}{2}$ km before dropping down east to the Bealach Choire a' Chait (726 m). The second half of the traverse goes up the west ridge of Sgurr nan Conbhairean, north to Tigh Mor na Seilge and down to Gleann na Ciche. Note that there is recently planted forest in this glen, so one should descend more or less due west to avoid a tiresome struggle through rows of trees.

The long range of mountains between Glen Affric and Glen Cannich starts in the east with one or two rounded hills of no great interest in the Fasnakyle Forest. The first of the high mountains is Toll Creagach (1053 m), a large rounded summit between Loch Beinn a' Mheadhoin

125

and Loch Mullardoch. Three kilometres west is Tom a' Choinich (1111 m) and 4 km further is Carn Eige (1183 m), the highest mountain in the Western Highlands. At this point the main ridge turns south for 1 km to Mam Sodhail (1181 m) while a subsidiary ridge goes north for 2 km to Beinn Fhionnlaidh, pronounced 'Benully', (1005 m). From Mam Sodhail the main ridge goes south-west and there is a steep drop to the Bealach Coire Ghaidheil (716 m), the lowest point on the range. Beyond this col is An Socach (920 m) and 3 km further west is Sgurr nan Ceathreamhnan (1151 m), a magnificent mountain of many peaks, ridges and corries. One of these peaks is Mullach na Dheiragain (982 m), which is situated far out along the north-north-east ridge of Sgurr nan Ceathreamhnan and is one of the remotest mountains in the Western Highlands. The west slopes of Sgurr nan Ceathreamhnan drop steeply into Gleann Gaorsaic, the end of this great range 18 km as the crow flies from Toll Creagach.

Toll Creagach (1053 m)

Toll Creagach is easily climbed from Loch Beinn a' Mheadhoin by Gleann nam Fiadh. A good path leads up the glen, and one should follow it until a convenient point is found to turn north and climb the hill. It may be that if forestry plantings extend across the south side of the hill it will be preferable to continue up the path beside the Allt Toll Easa to the bealach and climb the west ridge over the flat-topped West Top (952 m).

Tom a' Choinich (1111 m)

Tom a' Choinich can also be climbed from the Bealach Toll Easa (877 m) and can be easily combined with Toll Creagach. The path across this bealach was used in former days as a route between Affric Lodge and Benula Lodge, now submerged beneath the waters of Loch Mullardoch. The south-east ridge of Tom a' Choinich is also a good route of ascent or descent.

Carn Eige (1183 m), Mam Sodhail (1181 m)

Carn Eige and Mam Sodhail can probably best be climbed together in a grand circular traverse of the skyline of Gleann nam Fiadh, with Tom a' Choinich an optional extra for those feeling fit. Take the path up the

126

glen and, if Tom a' Choinich is to be included, continue up the Allt Toll Easa path for a short distance before climbing the south-east ridge of Tom a' Choinich. Follow the ridge west then south-west over Tom a' Choinich Beag (1029 m) and An Leth-chreag (1044 m) to reach the Garbh-bhealach (963 m). This point can be reached more easily by, instead of climbing Tom a' Choinich, continuing up Gleann nam Fiadh for a further 2 km and climbing the stalker's path up to the tiny lochan west of Coire Mhic Fhearchair, from which the bealach is a short climb. From there continue south-west along the ridge on a well made stalker's path; at one point on the steep ascent to Sron Garbh (1132 m) the path is almost a staircase up the rocky ridge. From Sron Garbh the ridge is fairly level for a kilometre, and there is a delightful section where the crest becomes very narrow and broken into some sharp pinnacles. The scramble along this crest is one of the best parts of the traverse, but it can be avoided without difficulty. The next rise is Stob a' Choire Dhomhain (1148 m), and from there a broad ridge leads to Carn Eige.

Beinn Fhionnlaidh (1005 m)

The ridge northwards from Carn Eige goes out to Beinn Fhionnlaidh over a minor Top, Stob Coire Lochan (917 m) and Munro baggers may well be tempted out along this ridge for there are no short ways to climb Beinn Fhionnlaidh, and the route over Carn Eige is as good as any from Glen Affric. Another possible route to this very remote mountain is from Alltbeithe youth hostel over the Bealach Coire Ghaidheil, down Gleann a' Choilich for a few kilometres and then diagonally up the south-west side.

One can also approach Beinn Fhionnlaidh from Glen Elchaig, having first obtained permission to drive as far as Loch na Leitreach. From there continue up the glen to Iron Lodge which is now rather misnamed as a rather ordinary looking house stands near the burned out ruins of the original lodge. From there follow the path over the pass near Loch an Droma to the foot of Gleann a' Choilich, the last part being trackless and rough going. Once across the Abhainn a' Choilich one climbs directly up the steep grassy slopes of Beinn Fhionnlaidh. This route takes one close to the little hut at the west end of Loch Mullardoch mentioned earlier in this chapter, and this hut is a good base for climbing Beinn Fhionnlaidh and other remote mountains in this area. One approach route that cannot be recommended is the walk along the south side of Loch Mullardoch from the dam; the going is extremely rough and tiring through deep heather. On the other hand, if one could hire a dingy and outboard motor at the dam, the approach to Beinn Fhionnlaidh is greatly simplified.

Returning to Carn Eige, the main ridge drops south-west then south across a col at 1045 m to reach Mam Sodhail. This summit was an important survey station in the primary triangulation of Scotland in the 1840's and its huge cairn was once over 7 m high. There was also a stone surveyors' shelter on the summit which, on a clear day, commands a widespread view over the northern half of Scotland. The completion of the traverse and return to the foot of Gleann nam Fiadh is best made by descending east-south-east along the grassy ridge over Mullach Cadha Rainich (993 m) to Sgurr na Lapaich (1036 m), a fine peak with a steep rocky face overlooking Affric Lodge. From the summit one can either descend north-east, steeply at first and then easily across the peaty moorland to return to Gleann nam Fiadh, or one can descend south-east to the path on the north side of Loch Affric and follow this east past Affric Lodge and a further 3 km to the day's starting point.

From the summit of Mam Sodhail the main ridge drops south-west for 1 km to a flat top, Ciste Dhubh (1100 m), and nearby a subsidiary ridge goes out south-east for 3 km to end above Loch Affric. An Tudair (1074 m) is the very shapely peak half way along this ridge which looks very fine from the south side of Loch Affric. The An Tudair and Sgurr na Lapaich ridges enclose Coire Leachavie, and a stalker's path up this corrie ends on the ridge about $\frac{1}{2}$ km south-west of Mam Sodhail. This path gives the shortest route to Mam Sodhail from the public road at the west end of Loch Beinn a' Mheadhoin.

Returning to Ciste Dhubh, the ridge continues south-west for $\frac{1}{2}$ km to the next minor summit, Carn Coulavie (1069 m), and there it turns south-east to Creag Coire nan Each (1056 m) before dropping towards Loch Affric. There is rather a discontinuity in the main ridge at Carn Coulavie, but the watershed drops steeply westwards to the Bealach Coire Ghaidheil, which is crossed by a path from Glen Affric to the head of Loch Mullardoch. The best route to Mam Sodhail from Alltbeithe is up this path to the bealach, then up Carn Coulavie and along the ridge to the summit.

An Socach (930 m)

An Socach is not named on the 1:50,000 Ordnance Survey map. It is a rather small peak between much higher neighbours, but it is fairly steep on three sides. It is most easily climbed from Alltbeithe by the path which starts behind the hostel and climbs to the bealach 1 km west of the summit. The small bump at the foot of the west ridge can be avoided, and a little time saved, if one leaves the path well below the bealach and climbs across the upper part of Coire na Cloiche directly towards the summit. Any other approach to An Socach, either from Affric Lodge or Cluanie Inn, is very long.

Sgurr nan Ceathreamhnan (1151 m), Mullach na Dheiragain (982 m)

Sgurr nan Ceathreamhnan, pronounced 'Kerranan', is the final mountain in the long range that we have been following, and it is one of the finest mountains in the Western Highlands. On the whole it has a more striking and graceful appearance than the rather featureless Carn Eige and Mam Sodhail, and had it an extra 35 m of height it could undoubtedly be regarded as the finest mountain in this part of the Highlands. A glance at the map will show the complex nature of Sgurr nan Ceathreamhnan with its many peaks, ridges and corries. The longest of these ridges goes from the summit north-eastwards for 6 km to end above Loch Mullardoch, and half way along this ridge is Mullach na Dheiragain which is classified as a separate mountain in Munro's Tables. Two other Tops on this very long ridge are Carn na Con Dhu (968 m) midway between Mullach na Dheiragain and Sgurr nan Ceathreamhnan, and Mullach Sithidh (973 m) at the point where the ridge divides north of Mullach na Dheiragain and forms two arms enclosing Coire Aird. Another ridge leads eastwards from the summit of Ceathreamhnan for 1½ km to Stob Coire nan Dearcag (c.940 m) and continues to An Socach, forming the main ridge between Affric and Cannich. Westwards from the summit there is a narrow level ridge for ½ km to the West Top (1143 m) from which three ridges radiate. The north ridge runs out over Stuc Bheag (1074 m) to Stuc Mor (1043 m) where it splits into two shoulders enclosing the Fraoch Choire with Loch an Fhraoich-choire enclosed by crags at its head. The north-west ridge forms a shoulder enclosing Coire Lochan, and the south ridge leads over Beinn an t-Socaich on the north side of Gleann Gniomhaidh.

By virtue of its remote position, the ascent of Sgurr nan Ceathreamhnan is a major expedition from any starting point, unless one happens to be staying at Alltbeithe youth hostel. In this case the ascent is short and easy, climbing north-west from the hostel to reach the east ridge of the mountain near the col just to the west of Stob Coire nan Dearcag.

The ascent from Cluanie Inn takes one north through An Caorann Mor to Alltbeithe and up the route just described, but one has to be fit and keen to continue to Mullach na Dheiragain knowing that every step out along this endless ridge has to be retraced.

The best route, in the author's opinion, that enables one to climb both Mullach na Dheiragain and Sgurr nan Ceathreamhnan is from Glen Elchaig, but one should get permission to drive to Loch na Leitreach and start from there. Continue up the glen to Iron Lodge, then east past Loch an Droma to the foot of Gleann Sithidh and up this glen to the end of the stalker's path near some fine cascading waterfalls. (In springtime if a lot of snow in Ceathreamhnan's northern corries is melting, or after heavy rain, this route may not be possible as there is no footbridge across the Abhainn Sithidh). Climb the steep grassy slope above the waterfalls to gain the north west shoulder of Mullach Sithidh which is followed over this Top and a further $\frac{1}{2}$ km to Mullach na Dheiragain. The long and in places rough ridge is followed over Carn na Con Dhu to the Bealach nan Daoine (840 m) and up the narrow rocky ridge to Sgurr nan Ceathreamhnan. Traverse the narrow summit ridge to the West Top and descend north-west along the smooth grassy ridge which encloses Coire Lochan. (Collectors of Tops may prefer to descend the north ridge over Stuc Bheag and Stuc Mor). Continue in a north-westerly direction down to Gleann Gaorsaic and follow the Abhainn Gaorsaic to the Falls of Glomach where the well marked path is joined and followed down to Loch na Leitreach. This makes a very fine finish to a superb day's hillwalking.

If one cannot get permission to drive to Loch na Leitreach then an alternative approach from Kintail is to start at Dorusduain in Strath Croe, cross the Bealach an Sgairne and continue along the Glen Affric path to the pass at the head of Gleann Gniomhaidh. From there one can climb north-eastwards to the col between Sgurr Gaorsaic and Sgurr nan Ceathreamhnan, and continue in the same direction to the West Top.

Walks and Paths

Glen Affric to Kintail. This cross-country walk is one of the finest in Scotland. It takes one through a wonderful variety of scenery from the forests of Glen Affric to the wild mountains of Kintail. One may elect to start walking at Cannich, in which case the first 18 km lead up the public road in Glen Affric, very beautiful but liable to be busy with cars in the tourist season. An alternative to avoid the traffic is the forest road on the south side of Loch Beinn a' Mheadhoin. However, most people start at the public road end just west of Loch Beinn a' Mheadhoin and continue along the private road to Affric Lodge and the right-of-way on the north side of Loch Affric. The path climbs some distance above the loch and its old pine forest, giving good views south-west to Mullach Fraoch-choire. Beyond Loch Affric the path continues through grassy flats by the river, reaching Alltbeithe youth hostel. At this point one has a choice of routes, either up Gleann Gniomhaidh and over the Bealach an Sgairne, or up the Fionngleann, past Camban bothy and down Gleann Lichd. Both these routes are described in the preceding chapter, and whichever one chooses the way goes through magnificent mountain scenery, leading ultimately to Strath Croe at the head of Loch Duich (28 km from Loch Beinn a' Mheadhoin to Loch Duich).

There are several tracks and paths through the extensive Guisachan Forest south of Loch Beinn a' Mheadhoin. One of these goes from Tomich to the small group of cottages at Cougie in the heart of the forest. From there one can continue west to reach Loch Affric, or continue south-west and south by a long path to reach Coire Dho and Ceannacroc Lodge in Glen Moriston. From Hilton Lodge, 4 km south-west of Tomich, a track goes south through the forest and across the moors to Dundreggan in Glen Moriston.

A good circular walk round Loch Affric can be made from the end of the public road in Glen Affric. Take the Forestry Commission road on the south side of the loch to Athnamulloch where there is a bridge across the River Affric, and return along the north side (17 km).

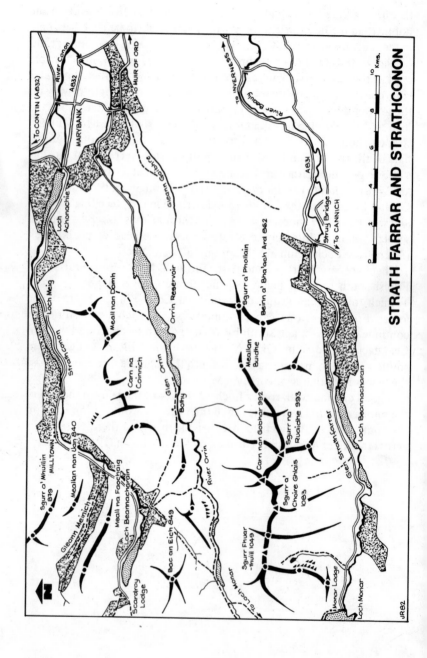

STRATH FARRAR AND STRATHCONON

62.   *The Five Sisters of Kintail from Loch Duich.*

63. *Sgurr nan Spainteach and Sgurr na Carnach from the slopes of Saileag above the Bealach an Lapain.*

64. *Saileag and Sgurr a' Bhealaich Dheirg from the west.*

65.   *The slabby east face of Sgurr nan Saighead.*

66.   *The North-West Peak of Sgurr nan Saighead.*

67.   *Sgurr nan Saighead, Sgurr Fhuaran and Sgurr na Carnach from the north-west.*

68. Glenlicht House below the north-eastern ridges of the Five Sisters.

69. In Strath Croe, looking up Gleann Lichd to Sgurr a' Bhealaich Dheirg and Saileag.

70.   The east face of Sgurr a' Choire Ghairbh at the west end of Beinn Fhada.

71.   On the Plaide Mhor, the flat summit plateau of Beinn Fhada, looking west to
      Beinn Sgritheall.

72. On the Leac Beag of Boc Beag, looking towards the Cuillin Hills on Skye.

73. The approach to Boc Beag from the west.

11

Glen Cannich and Strathfarrar

Carn nan Gobhar (992 m) 182344
Sgurr na Lapaich (1150 m) 161351
An Riabhachan (1129 m) 134345
An Socach (1069 m) 100333
Sgurr na Ruaidhe (993 m) 289426
Carn nan Gobhar (992 m) 273439
Sgurr a' Choire Ghlais (1083 m) 259430
Sgurr Fhuar-thuill (1049 m) 236437

Munro's Tables, Section 12

MAPS: Ordnance Survey 1:50,000 (2nd Series) Sheets 25 and 26.

The area to be described in this chapter is the northward extension of that dealt with in the last chapter, and it has many of the same characteristics as the Affric mountains. The lie of the land is dominated by the long east-west glens and their intervening ranges of mountains. These glens rise far to the west, not far from the Killilan and Glen Carron mountains, and drain to the Beauly and Cromarty firths. There are four such glens: Glen Cannich, the southern boundary of the area described in this chapter, is wooded in its lower part, and the upper part is filled by the long narrow Loch Mullardoch. Next to the north, Glen Strathfarrar is a very fine glen, second only to Glen Affric in the variety and beauty of its scenery which includes some lovely birch and pine woods. The higher reaches of the glen are more barren and the greatly enlarged Loch Monar is almost the twin of Loch Mullardoch over the hills to the south. Next is Glen Orrin, very desolate and devoid of road or habitation. Finally, there is Strathconon, the northern boundary of the area described in this chapter; like Strathfarrar it has a great variety of scenery and is the most populous of these glens, having a good deal

K

of farm and forest land in its lower half from the little village of Milltown down to the foot of the strath.

The main mountains in the area of this chapter are in two east-west ranges, one on the north side of Loch Mullardoch, and the other on the north side of Glen Strathfarrar. Elsewhere, particularly in the east of the area on both sides of Glen Orrin, there is a vast expanse of rolling hills and moorland which have neither the character nor the height to attract climbers away from the higher western mountains.

There are four possible routes of access to these mountains. Firstly up Glen Cannich to the Loch Mullardoch dam; secondly up the private road in Glen Strathfarrar to the Loch Monar dam; thirdly up Strathconon to Scardroy and finally (and most remotely) up Glen Elchaig.

The road up Glen Strathfarrar is private, and a gate across the road near Struy is normally locked, access being controlled by the owners of the estates up the glen. With the agreement of the landowners, the Nature Conservancy Council administer a small Nature Reserve in the lower part of the glen. Permission to drive up the glen and a key for the gate is obtainable from the local representative of the Nature Conservancy Council whose house is beside the locked gate, and one should call at the house or telephone beforehand (046 376 260). The hours between which permission is normally granted to drive up the glen are at present:—

> Weekdays (except Tuesdays), 9.00 a.m. to 6.00 p.m.
> Sundays, 1.00 p.m. to 6.00 p.m.
> Tuesdays, no access.

In winter months the Nature Conservancy Council representative may not always be at home, and it is therefore advisable to telephone beforehand.

The Glen Elchaig approach is useful for the mountains at the west end of Loch Mullardoch, but the road is private beyond Killilan. Permission may be obtained to drive beyond Killilan to Loch na Leitreach, at which point the mountains are within reasonable walking distance.

Accommodation is available at Cannich, hotel, youth hostel and bed and breakfast; Struy, hotel; Strathconon, hotel at Milltown and in the peripheral towns such as Beauly, Muir of Ord and Conon Bridge. The small hut at the west end of Loch Mullardoch mentioned in the last chapter is a good remote shelter (if it has not fallen down) and there is a remote but comfortable bothy at Luipmaldrig, a few kilometres up the River Orrin from the Orrin Reservoir. As mentioned in the previous chapter it may be possible to get bed and breakfast accommodation at Cozac Lodge near the Mullardoch dam.

The range on the north side of Loch Mullardoch consists of four mountains: Carn nan Gobhar (992 m), Sgurr na Lapaich (1150 m), An Riabhachan (1129 m) and An Socach (1069 m). They form a more or less continuous ridge about 10 km long as the crow flies from east to west. The general impression of these hills is that they have few outstanding features. Sgurr na Lapaich has a well-defined pointed summit which with its greater height makes it the most easily recognisable peak of the group. An Riabhachan appears as a long flat ridge to which An Socach is a lower western extension. On their south side these mountains rise without any intervening heights from Loch Mullardoch in a series of open grassy corries. On the north side they are much more remote from Strathfarrar and Loch Monar, and only where the long Gleann Innis an Loichel penetrates from Strathfarrar towards the north side of Sgurr na Lapaich is there a good route of approach from that side. At the head of this glen there is a fine craggy corrie under the north-east ridge of An Riabhachan which is one of the finest features of this group of mountains.

The approach along the north side of Loch Mullardoch from the dam is straightforward if not exactly easy going all the way. The raising of the level of the loch has not only submerged the old Cozac and Benula lodges, but also the road along the north side of the loch which gave access to them. Now there are some sections where a footpath remains, and others where one has to make do with sheep tracks contouring along the hillside above the loch. Eight kilometres along the loch, on its north side, a house has recently been built at the foot of the Allt Socrach. The bothy nearby used to be available for climbers and walkers, but this may no longer be the case. One should enquire locally.

Carn nan Gobhar (992 m)

Carn nan Gobhar is easily reached from the road end at the Mullardoch dam. Continue along the north side of the loch and take the stalker's path up the Allt Mullardoch into Coire an t-Sith. One can include the eastern Top, Creag Dubh (946 m) by climbing due north, and then one goes west-south-west along a broad ridge to Carn nan Gobhar, whose summit is about 200 m north of the cairn.

Sgurr na Lapaich (1150 m)

Sgurr na Lapaich is the highest and finest mountain of this group, having a steep summit cone and some fine corries on its east flank. The main ridge of the mountain runs from south to north, there is a lower Top, Sgurr nan Clachan Geala (1095 m) 1 km south of the summit, and beyond this Top there is a fairly level ridge, Braigh a' Choire Bhig (1011 m). Two routes are possible for the ascent of Sgurr na Lapaich, one from Loch Mullardoch and the other from Glen Strathfarrar. For the former, walk along the north side of the loch past the little plantation above the site of the former Cozac Lodge to the foot of the Allt Taige. It is then a matter of personal choice as to whether one takes the stalker's path up the burn into the Glas Toll to climb the south-east ridge of Sgurr nan Clachan Geala, or continues up to the bealach at the head of the corrie to climb the east ridge of Sgurr na Lapaich, or climbs the long ridge to the west of the Allt Taige over Mullach a' Ghlas-thuill and Braigh a' Choire Bhig.

From Glen Strathfarrar one should take the road up the Uisge Misgeach to the power station, and from there climb south-west up the broad shoulder of Sgurr na Lapaich, over the small top called Rudha na Spreidhe (c.1050 m). The last part of this route is along the north ridge which with the east ridge encloses the steep upper part of the Garbh-choire. One could equally well ascend the mountain from the Uisge Misgeach by this corrie, and in winter there is the possibility of a climb on the upper cliffs near the summit. One such route is *Deer-Gran Gully* (130 m, Grade III) by D. Langudge and J. Mackenzie, which takes a central line up the cliffs below the east ridge. The east face of Sgurr nan Clachan Geala overlooking Loch Tuill Bhearnach is steep and rocky and might give a good winter climb.

An Riabhachan (1129 m)

The next mountain to the west is An Riabhachan, a long level ridge with grassy corries to the north and south. The highest part of this ridge is about 2 km long, flat, broad and mossy. The summit is near the middle, with the North-East Top (c.1120 m) at one end and the South-West Top (1086 m) at the other. At the east end of the mountain a fairly narrow ridge drops from the North-East Top to the Bealach Toll an Lochain (c.820 m), and on the north side of this ridge there are some steep crags, called the Creagan Toll an Lochain, above Loch Mor and Loch Beag.

The only recorded climb on An Riabhachan has been done on these crags, *Spindrift Gully* (200 m, Grade II) by D. Smith and J. G. Stewart. The gully cuts straight up through the right hand half of the prominent rock face just west of the Bealach Toll an Lochain. It contains one pitch and is steep in its upper half. (S.M.C.J., Vol. XXIX, No. 162, p. 408).

From the South-West Top the main ridge of An Riabhachan is quite narrow and drops in two stages westwards, with a small intermediate knoll, to the Bealach a' Bholla (901 m).

Like Sgurr na Lapaich, An Riabhachan can be climbed either from Cannich or Strathfarrar and both can be combined in a single expedition. The walking distances to and from the mountain are quite long, for example at least 13 km from the Mullardoch dam. The hire of a dinghy and outboard motor would simplify the approach. From the dam, if one is not doing Sgurr na Lapaich as well, there is an 8 km walk along the lochside to the house at the foot of the Allt Socrach. The stalker's path up this burn is followed to its end and one then has to make a way up grassy slopes directly to the summit.

From Glen Strathfarrar one should go to the end of the road in Gleann Innis an Loichel, continue up the stalker's path to Loch Mor in the Toll an Lochain and climb steeply to the bealach at the foot of An Riabhachan's east ridge. This ridge gives a pleasant climb to the summit. The descent by this route requires caution in winter on the steep slope on the north side of the Bealach Toll an Lochain.

An Socach (1069 m)

An Socach, which (like its namesake to Glen Affric) is not named on the Ordnance Survey map, is even more remote than An Riabhachan, being a continuation of that mountain westwards beyond the Bealach a' Bholla. The summit is near the middle of a crescent-shaped ridge which encloses the head of Coire Mhaim. This rather featureless corrie is on the south-east of An Socach and it has some not very steep crags and buttresses at its head. On all other sides the flanks of An Socach are grassy and not very interesting. A long shoulder goes out to the south-west enclosing Coire Lungard.

Most hill-walkers will try to combine the traverse of An Socach with An Riabhachan. In this case it is very straightforward to continue westwards from the latter across the Bealach a' Bholla and up the short ridge to An Socach. To return to Loch Mullardoch, one should continue south-east round the broad ridge, descending to the flat ground near the foot of Coire Mhaim. The floor of this corrie is a terrible maze of dissected peat hags, and any route up or down the middle of the corrie is not advised. The path down the Allt Coire a' Mhaim is, however, easier going and brings one down to the house by Loch Mullardoch and 8 km more of hard walking back to the dam unless one is lucky enough to have a boat waiting by the shore.

An alternative approach to An Socach is from Glen Elchaig. If one has permission to drive to Loch na Leitreach, then the walking distance to the mountain is slightly less than the distance from the Mullardoch dam, with the added advantage of easier going along the road to Iron Lodge and up the path to Loch Mhoicean, beyond which one can climb directly up the west side of the mountain by a long steep grass slope.

The shortest route of all to An Socach is from the little hut at the west end of Loch Mullardoch, but one may have problems crossing the mudflats at the head of the loch unless a long detour to the west is made.

In the desolate country north of An Socach there rises An Cruachan (706 m), a hill of more interest to geologists than climbers. It has some unusual rocks for the area, including a variety containing graphite. The only feasible route of approach, and it is a long one, is from Iron Lodge.

Sgorr na Diollaid (818 m)

Near the east end of Glen Cannich, Sgorr na Diollaid is the highest of several low hills which separate the lower part of that glen from Glen Strathfarrar. Its rocky top is a conspicuous landmark, but gives no real climbing. The easiest ascent is from the south, starting at the bridge near Muchrachd in Glen Cannich and climbing due north. The true summit of the hill is a crest of rocky knobs about 200 m long, the highest point being at the north end. The traverse of the ridge gives an easy scramble.

The North Strathfarrar Ridge; Sgurr a' Choire Ghlais (1083 m) etc.

The mountains on the north side of Glen Strathfarrar form a much more compact group than those just described, and they are very accessible from the private road up the glen to Loch Monar. It is perfectly feasible to traverse all four mountains in a day, and they will be described accordingly. The three eastern mountains, **Sgurr na Ruaidhe** (993 m), **Carn nan Gobhar** (992 m) and **Sgurr a' Choire Ghlais** (1083 m), are all fairly rounded with smooth contours, but the ridge becomes narrower as it goes west over **Sgurr Fhuar-thuill** (1049 m) to ats western Top, Sgurr na Fearstaig (1015 m). There the ridge turns south and goes over the unnamed Pt. 880 m to Sgurr na Muice (891 m), a peak with a very steep rocky east face which makes it the most striking of the group. Continuing south, there is a fine little hill Beinn na Muice (693 m) which shows up as a prominent steep cone when seen from along Loch Monar to the west.

Apart from the east face of Sgurr na Muice, the adjacent south-east corrie of Sgurr na Fearstaig has a line of crags below Pt. 880 m, and the north side of the Sgurr Fhuar-thuill ridge has some fine corries, of which the Fhuar-thuill Mhoir is probably the finest, but none of these corries have particularly steep or rocky headwalls. Elsewhere the slopes of these mountains are smooth and grassy, giving easy walking, particularly on the broad ridges. The north sides of these hills drop to the very desolate upper reaches of Glen Orrin, and most people make the ascent from Glen Strathfarrar in the south.

The traverse of the four Munros can be started 2 km east of the Loch Monar dam, at the foot of the Allt Toll a' Mhuic, and one follows the footpath up the burn below the steep face of Sgurr na Muice. In summer conditions this face gives a good scramble; the structure of the crag is characterised by several big ledges slanting up from south to north, with steep rock bands between them. It is possible to find a route up the face, with some traversing along the ledges if necessary. The standard is Moderate to Very Difficult, depending on route finding skill. Once on the summit of Sgurr na Muice the ridge is followed north. For those who do not fancy this rather steep scramble, the path continues to Loch Toll a' Mhuic and then tends to disappear in the corrie beyond. Higher up the path reappears on the west side of the corrie and it traverses the steep headwall below Sgurr na Fearstaig to reach the main ridge just east of this summit. The next part of the ridge over Sgurr Fhuar-thuill to Creag Ghorm a' Bhealaich is quite narrow, with steep drops on the north to the Fhuar-thuill Mhoir and Coire na Sguile.

At Sgurr a' Choire Ghlais, the highest peak of the group, the character of the hills changes and they become more rounded. Carn nan Gobhar and Sgurr na Ruaidhe are both rather flat-topped, and the ridges between them are broad. In thick weather some careful compass work may be needed for the connecting ridges do not run east to west, but twist and turn, at one point going south to north. From Sgurr na Ruaidhe the return to Glen Strathfarrar is best made by descending the broad shoulder of the hill south-west into Coire Mhuillich to reach the stalker's path in the lower part of this corrie and return to the road about 6 km east of one's starting point.

The traverse of these mountains can be made from the north, though the approach from that direction is obviously much longer than the Strathfarrar approach. It has the attraction, however, of taking one through some very remote and unknown country at the head of Glen Orrin. From Inverchoran in Strathconon a path leads south-west to Loch na Caoidhe in Glen Orrin, and from there one climbs south and then up the north-west ridge of Sgurr na Fearstaig. The best descent route from the eastern end of the ridge is from Carn nan Gobhar north to the bridge over the River Orrin below the impressive Creag a' Ghlastail, from where a forestry road leads back to Inverchoran. Bothy-dwellers can use Luipmaldrig, a few kilometres down the River Orrin, as a base for hill-walking in this area.

The face of Sgurr na Muice overlooking Loch Toll a' Mhuic, and the continuation of this face northwards to the col south of Pt. 880 m has given several winter climbs to J. Mackenzie and his companions. On the approach up the Allt Toll a' Mhuic one can see in good winter conditions two parallel ice-falls on the south-east side of Sgurr na Muice. Both have been climbed. The left-hand one is *Best Back* (150 m, Grade III/IV). A pitch leads to the lower mass of ice which gives 70° climbing. The ice above steepens to a bulge, above which easier climbing leads to the top. The right-hand ice-fall is *Streaky* (150 m, Grade III/IV). (S.M.C.J., Vol. XXXI, No. 169, p. 280 and No. 170, p. 409).

Further up the corrie, beyond the nose of Sgurr na Muice, the cliff extends towards the col just south of Pt. 880 m. To the left of this col there are two gullies. *Trotter's Gully* (250 m, Grade III) is a long curved gully between shallow walls. On the first ascent the left fork was climbed to a cornice finish. Further left is the shallower *Pigsty Gully* (250 m, Grade II) which has a prominent cleft top. Minor pitches lead to the cleft which may be blocked by a large cornice. (S.M.C.J., Vol. XXXI, No. 169, p. 280 and Vol. XXXII, No. 172, p. 155).

The slope up to the col referred to above is an easy route of ascent or descent. To its north, the east face of Pt. 880 m has a series of corners giving short Grade II/III routes. At the right end of this face there are two short gullies, and to their left there is a well-defined steep groove. This is the line of *Enchanter's Nightshade* (100 m, Grade III) climbed by J. Mackenzie. The groove is slabby on the right and forms an ice-fall, which is climbed, followed by another steep groove to the big cornice which is outflanked on the left by a snow arête. To the left of this groove is the long slanting ramp of *Sea-Pink Gully* (120 m, Grade II).

Walks and Paths

The three classic long distance cross-country walks in the area of this chapter are Glen Cannich to Glen Elchaig, Glen Strathfarrar to Glen Carron and Strathconon to Glen Carron. These three routes rank with the Glen Affric to Kintail walk described in the last chapter for length and general character, although none of them quite matches the scenic quality of the Glen Affric route. Only the Glen Cannich route will be described here, the other two being reserved for the next chapter.

Glen Cannich to Glen Elchaig. If the walk is started at Cannich village, the first 15 km are along the road to the Loch Mullardoch dam. The continuation along the north side of the loch is rough going in places, particularly towards the west end. Eventually near the west end of the loch a path is found which improves as it goes over the low pass near Loch an Droma and descends to Iron Lodge. From there the road is followed down Glen Elchaig. The total distance from Cannich to Killilan is 46 km.

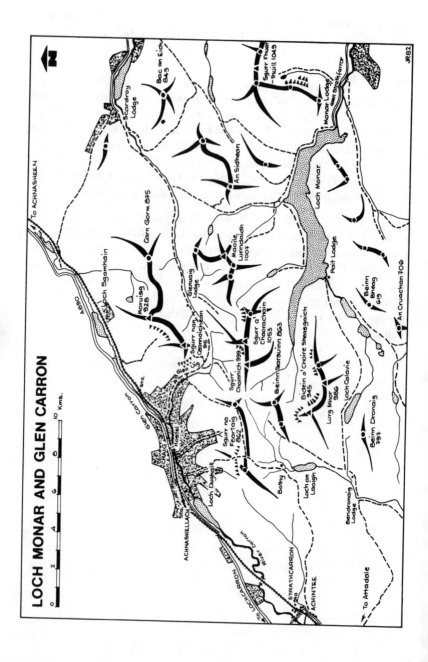

LOCH MONAR AND GLEN CARRON

12

Glen Carron, Killilan and West Monar

Sguman Coinntich (879 m) 977304
Faochaig (868 m) 022317
Aonach Buidhe (899 m) 057325
Moruisg (928 m) 102500
Sgurr nan Ceannaichean (915 m) 087481
Sgurr Choinnich (999 m) 076446
Sgurr a' Chaorachain (1053 m) 088448
Bidean an Eoin Deirg (1046 m) 103443
Maoile Lunndaidh (1007 m) 135458
Bidein a' Choire Sheasgaich (945 m) 049413
Lurg Mhor (986 m) 065405
Sgurr a' Mhuilinn (879 m) 264557

MAP: Ordnance Survey 1:50,000 (2nd Series) Sheets 25 and 26.

The north-west perimeter of the Western Highlands as defined by this guide book is formed by Glen Carron and Strath Bran, the long wide valley which crosses Scotland in a great arc from the Cromarty Firth to Loch Carron. This final chapter describes the mountains on the south-east side of this long valley as far east as the watersheds at the head of the long glens described in the previous chapter. Thus the eastern boundary of the area is defined by Loch Long, Glen Elchaig and its extension north-east to Pait Lodge, across Loch Monar to Coire Fionnarach and north through this corrie to the River Meig, finally following this river down Strathconon to the Cromarty Firth. Much of this eastern boundary passes through country as remote as any in the Western Highlands.

The area can be subdivided into four parts, each with its own characteristics. In the south-east the Killilan Forest is a well defined group of hills encircled by the rivers Ling and Elchaig and their tributaries. The south-west corner between Loch Carron and the River

Ling as far north-east as the Attadale estate is rough undulating moorland, forested in places, but having no hills of any interest. The only feature of climbing importance in this area is the line of crags on the hillside opposite Plockton village, but although some climbing has been done on these crags, nothing has been recorded. The central part of the area described in this chapter, lying between Glen Carron and the head of Loch Monar, is the most mountainous part, containing seven Munros and nearly all the hill-walking interest. Finally, the north-eastern part between Strath Bran and Strathconon has one outstanding mountain, Sgurr a' Mhuilinn, and some low-lying crags of rock-climbing interest, but is otherwise undulating moorland and low hills.

Access to the mountains is most conveniently made as follows:—For the Killilan hills one can leave the A87 road to Kyle of Lochalsh at Ardelve and drive up the west side of Loch Long to the end of the public road at Killilan, and possibly a further 8 km up the private road in Glen Elchaig. For the mountains in the Achnashellach, Glencarron and West Monar estates one should leave the A890 road in Glen Carron at Achnashellach or Craig. For Sgurr a' Mhuilinn one should drive up Strathconon to Strathanmore; it is possible to continue up the strath to the end of the public road at Scardroy Lodge at which point the Glencarron and West Monar peaks are not too far distant at the head of Gleann Fhiodhaig. All other lines of approach from the east, for example from the roadend in Glen Strathfarrar along the length of Loch Monar, are very much longer and may involve some rough going.

There are a few public transport services which can be used to reach this area. The bus services from Glasgow and Inverness to Kyle of Lochalsh pass through Ardelve, and the railway from Inverness to Kyle of Lochalsh goes through Strath Bran and Glen Carron with stations at Achnasheen, Achnashellach and Strathcarron. A post-bus service connects Muir of Ord on this railway with Strathconon.

Accommodation for climbers is mostly available in the south-west corner of the area, in the villages of Dornie, Ardelve and Lochcarron where there are hotels, bed and breakfast houses and caravans to let. There is an open hostel (not SYHA) at Craig, $3\frac{1}{2}$ km east of Achnashellach which is popular with climbers and walkers. Achnasheen has two hotels, but it is rather far from the mountains. In Strathconon there is a hotel at Milltown, and at Scardroy Lodge a few kilometres further up the strath it may be possible to get accommodation at the bothy. Two other bothies deserve mention; both have been renovated by the Mountain Bothies Association and give very good but simple shelter in the heart of the mountains. Bearnais bothy (marked but not named on the Ordnance Survey map at (021430) was restored as a memorial to the climber Eric Beard, and Maol-bhuidhe (053360) is an extremely isolated cottage by the headwaters of the River Ling which is useful if one is approaching the mountainous heart of the area from Glen Elchaig as it is most easily reached by the path which strikes northwards from Iron Lodge in that glen.

Sguman Coinntich (879 m), Aonach Buidhe (899 m), Faochaig (868 m)

The three principal mountains in the Killilan Forest are Sguman Coinntich, Faochaig and Aonach Buidhe. They are rather massive hills with great rounded shoulders, broad ridges and big corries only one of which, that on the east side of Faochaig, is particularly steep. There might appear to be some interesting crags, particularly Creag Mhor, a northern spur of Sguman Coinntich, but no climbing has been recorded on this or any other of the Killilan hills.

Sguman Coinntich is a horseshoe-shaped mountain surrounding the west facing Choire Mhoir at the head of Loch Long. The summit is on the south arm of the horseshoe, and Ben Killilan (Sgurr na Cloiche, 753 m) is on the north arm. The simplest ascent is directly up the stalkers' path in Choire Mhoir to the Bealach Mhic Beathain from which the highest point is only 1 km distant. The shortest route to Faochaig is the stalker's path from Carnach in Glen Elchaig up the Allt Domhain, and Aonach Buidhe is best climbed from Iron Lodge directly up its broad south ridge.

Going north from Killilan to the Attadale estate across the River Ling, one comes to Beinn Dronaig (797 m), a featureless hill overlooking Loch Calavie and Bendronaig Lodge. This lodge is very isolated, being linked to Attadale on Loch Carron by 12 km of very rough and tortuous track which make a very long approach route to the high mountains north of the lodge.

Turning now to these mountains which lie in the centre of the area described in this chapter, it is appropriate to start at Craig in Glen Carron. From there one can go up through the forest into Glen Uig (named the Allt a' Chonais on the Ordnance Survey map), and 6 km up this glen, where it curves round to the east, one is at the heart of these mountains. On the north side of the glen steep grassy slopes rise to Sgurr nan Ceannaichean and Moruisg, to the south is the rocky corrie between Sgurr Choinnich and Sgurr a' Chaorachain, and further away, beyond the intervening ridges, are the other peaks grouped in a great cirque round the west end of Loch Monar. With the exception of Sgurr nan Ceannaichean and Moruisg, these are all rather remote mountains; certainly they are well hidden from Glen Carron behind the lower, nearer hills and only from Lochcarron village can one glimpse a few of the higher summits above the Attadale ridges.

Sgurr nan Ceannaichean (915 m), Moruisg (928 m)

Sgurr nan Ceannaichean and Moruisg rise directly above Glen Carron, and are the most accessible mountains of this group. The west face of Sgurr nan Ceannaichean which rises above Glen Uig is very steep and riven by two prominent gullies, the right-hand (south) one being particularly deep-cut. The corrie between the two hills on the Glen Carron side, the Coire Toll nam Bian, has a steep headwall, but it is broken rock and grass and offers no climbing possibilities. Moruisg itself is rather a featureless hill with a broad undulating ridge running eastwards from the summit for several kilometres over Carn Gorm. On the north side of this ridge is the large open corrie drained by the Allt Gharagain, and on the south side steep grassy slopes drop to Gleann Fhiodhaig.

The traverse of the two mountains can most easily be made from Glen Carron, starting at the footbridge across the River Carron 1 km downstream from Loch Sgamhain. Follow the footpath towards Coire Toll nam Bian for almost 2 km and then climb the steepening grassy slopes of Moruisg in an easterly direction, avoiding the deep gullies which cut this hillside, and reach the flat, mossy summit. There is a very easy walk south and then south-west to the col from where the steeper ridge of Sgurr nan Ceannaichean leads to the flat top on which there are two cairns, the true summit being the smaller one overlooking the east corrie. The return is down the north ridge until it is easy to cross to the right bank of the Alltan na Feola and rejoin the path that leads back to the day's starting point.

Sgurr nan Ceannaichean can also be easily climbed from Glen Uig. Leaving the good track which leads up this glen 1 km beyond the gate at the tree line, one can climb the steep north-west shoulder of the mountain which is not as rocky as the Ordnance Survey map indicates. The return to Glen Uig can be made down the stalker's path on the grassy south side of the mountain, thus making a short and simple traverse.

The two gullies on the west face of Sgurr nan Ceannaichean have both been explored, but it is uncertain if either has been climbed in its entirety. The narrower north gully has several pitches which were avoided on the first ascent, and the big south gully has a large chockstone pitch. It is doubtful if these gullies are worth attention in summer as there is too much vegetation, scree and loose rock. However, in a hard winter they would be worth renewed exploration.

Sgurr Choinnich (999 m), Sgurr a' Chaorachain (1053 m), Bidean an Eoin Deirg (1046 m)

The three mountains Sgurr Choinnich, Sgurr a' Chaorachain and Bidean an Eoin Deirg form a high ridge running east to west between Glen Uig and the head of Loch Monar, and they can best be described together, particularly as they make a very good traverse. Sgurr Choinnich has a narrow summit ridge on whose north side steep cliffs drop into the fine unnamed corrie above Glen Uig. The top, marked by a very small cairn, is near the middle of the fairly level summit ridge. Sgurr a' Chaorachain is a more rounded hill, particularly on its north side, and its stony summit is crowned by a large cairn. From it a fairly level stony ridge leads east-south-east to Bidean an Eoin Deirg which is the finest peak of the trio with a very steep rocky buttress dropping north from the summit.

For the west to east traverse one should take the path from Glen Uig south-west to the Bealach Bhearnais and climb Sgurr Choinnich by its pleasant west ridge, which is grassy with occasional little rock steps. The continuation of the traverse is straightforward and calls for no special description; in misty weather one should look carefully for the sudden turn in the ridge a short distance south-east of Sgurr Choinnich, otherwise one may unintentionally include Sgurr na Conbhaire in the traverse. From Bidean an Eoin Deirg the descent northwards cannot be recommended as an easy way down, and it is better to return to Sgurr a' Chaorachain and descend its north ridge, but even its lower part is steep and there are crags (unmarked on the Ordnance Survey map) on the north side of Sron na Frianich.

Maoile Lunndaidh (1007 m)

To the east of the group just described lies Maoile Lunndaidh, a massive mountain between Loch Monar and Gleann Fhiodhaig. The summit is a narrow curving plateau between two deep corries, the

Fuar-tholl Mor and the Toll a' Choin, and there are three tops. The name Maoile Lunndaidh refers to the north-east top; the centre top is more or less the same height and is known as Creag Toll a' Choin, and the western top is Carn nam Fiaclan (996 m). The drops between these three tops is very slight, and in the latest edition of Munro's Tables Creag Toll a' Choin has been deleted as a Top. The finest feature of the mountain is the Fuar-tholl Mor, a deeply cut corrie enclosed by steep walls and holding three little lochans in its depths. The Toll a' Choin is another fine corrie ringed by crags, but elswhere the slopes of the mountain are grassy.

Maoile Lunndaidh is nearly equidistant from three possible starting points for its ascent; Craig in Glen Carron, Scardroy in Strathconon and the Loch Monar dam at the head of Glen Strathfarrar. The first of these is probably the shortest approach, particularly if one has permission to drive up to the gate at the tree line in Glen Uig. From there one walks right up the glen and 1 km beyond the watershed. Before reaching Glenuaig Lodge one should bear south-east to cross An Crom-allt and climb the steep north-west slopes of Carn nam Fiaclan, and so round the ridge to the highest point. The return can be varied by descending due north from this point to the flat col at 750 m, and then dropping down westwards to cross the stream flowing out of the Fuar-tholl Mor and, continuing in the same direction, regain the track to Glen Uig.

Maoile Lunndaidh can be combined with the three mountains previously described in a very good long day's hillwalking. It is probably best to climb Maoile Lunndaidh first and descend west from Carn nam Fiaclan to the col at 600 m below Bidean an Eoin Deirg whose north face gives a steep and in places rocky climb. Thereafter the traverse to Sgurr a' Chaorachain and Sgurr Choinnich is straightforward, as already described. The descent to Glen Uig from the col between these two peaks is perfectly easy.

The other two possible routes to Maoile Lunndaidh can be briefly described as follows:—From Scardroy the path up the River Meig and the Allt an Amise is followed to the watershed at the head of this stream, from where Maoile Lunndaidh is just over 2 km distant to the west. From the east end of Loch Monar one takes the private road to Monar Lodge and follows the very good path on the north side of the loch and its continuation up the Allt Toll a' Choin, finally climbing one of the bounding ridges of this corrie.

The only recorded climb on Maoile Lunndaidh is in the Toll a'

74. *Eilean Donnan Castle.*

75. *Ben Killilan and Sguman Coinntich from Loch Long.*

76.   *The Falls of Glomach.*

77. *Looking through the Bealach an Sgairne to Mullach Fraoch-choire.*

78. *Camban bothy in the Fionngleann, looking towards Sgurr a' Bhealaich Dheirg.*

79. *A'Chralaig from one of the pinnacles on the south ridge of Mullach Fraoch-choire.*

80. *Sgurr nan Conbhairean from the south-east.*

81. *Sgurr na Lapaich from Glen Affric.*

82. *On the pass between Glen Elchaig and Loch Mullardoch, looking towards Beinn Fhionnlaidh.*

83. *Looking north from Beinn Fhionnlaidh to An Socach.*

84. *Bidein a' Choire Sheasgaich from the west ridge of Sgurr Choinnich.*

85. *Looking up the Allt a' Chonais to Sgurr a' Chaorachain and Sgurr Choinnich. Prolonged dry weather has reduced the stream to a trickle.*

86. *The west face of Sgurr nan Ceannaichean.*

87. *Sgurr na Lapaich from Glen Strathfarrar, looking up the Uisge Misgeach.*

88. *A warning to climbers in Strathconon.*

DEER IN THESE HILLS ARE
SHOT FROM MID AUGUST–FEBRUARY
FOR SPORT, MEAT & GOVERNMENT
DEER CONTROL POLICY.
   WALKERS ARE THEREFORE
WARNED THAT RAMBLING ON
HIGH GROUND AT THIS TIME
CAN SERIOUSLY UPSET LARGE
AREAS FOR DEERSTALKING AND
CAN BE DANGEROUS.

NO CAMPING AREA.

Choin; it is *Mica Ridge* (100 m, Difficult), climbed by A. Watson and A. Watson (senior) in May 1954. On the left of the corrie there is a steep vegetatious wall. The route is up the first definite ridge to the right of this wall, and it stays close to the crest, traversing by steps and ledges on the steep right side. On the first ascent there was a snow comb and a big cornice at the top. (S.M.C.J., Vol. XXV, No. 146, p. 357).

Bidein a' Choire Sheasgaich (945 m), Lurg Mhor (986 m)

The last two Munros in the area being described are Bidein a' Choire Sheasgaich and Lurg Mhor. (The name of the latter mountain is shown on the Ordnance Survey map as referring to the southern shoulder, but it does apply to the mountain as a whole). These two peaks form a long curving ridge round the south-west side of the head of Loch Monar, and the ridge of Lurg Mhor continues for a few kilometres eastwards over Meall Mor to end above Pait Lodge. They are both very remote and fine peaks; Bidein, for example, appears as a prominent sharp-pointed summit when seen from the north or south, and the ridge between the two tops of Lurg Mhor is very narrow. All in all, these are two mountains whose ascent is particularly highly prized by hill-walkers.

The most practicable approach routes start at Achnashellach and Craig in Glen Carron, and Bearnais bothy is well placed if one wants to explore the peaks in a more leisurely way than is possible in a one-day expedition. The following route should be within the capability of most reasonably fit hill-walkers wanting to do both peaks in a single day:—From Craig follow the track up the Allt a' Chonais (Glen Uig) for about 6 km, and then the stalkers' path to the Bealach Bhearnais. Now traverse Beinn Tharsuinn (863 m), the west peak need not be climbed before dropping down to the Bealach an Sgoltaidh. (Here again the Ordnance Survey map appears to have misplaced the name). The north ridge of Bidein a' Choire Sheasgaich rises very steeply above the bealach, its lowest part encircled by cliffs, and a steep scramble up and rightwards leads to a more level section of the ridge where a tiny lochan is perched at the edge of the cliffs. The ascent continues without difficulty over a small top to the summit. There follows a fairly long descent down the south-east ridge and up the west ridge of Lurg Mhor. The lower summit of this mountain (974 m) is about $\frac{3}{4}$ km distant to the east, and the narrow connecting ridge has one section of slight difficulty which cannot be easily avoided. The return to Craig may be made by the outward route, with a good deal of up and downhill work; alternatively, it is quite feasible (given good visibility) to avoid some of this climbing by descending north-north-east from the col between Lurg Mhor and Bidein and traversing across the east side of Beinn Tharsuinn to reach the Bealach Bhearnais. Although this may save time, it can only be recommended with reservation.

The alternative way to climb these two mountains is to take more than one day and stay at Bearnais bothy. The shortest and (in the author's opinion) pleasantest route to the bothy is from Achnashellach across the River Carron, up the path on the east side of Coire Leiridh, over the flat and featureless col west of Sgurr na Feartag and down to the bothy, which has a very isolated situation in the desolate Bearneas glen. The Abhainn Bhearnais may be difficult to cross in wet weather, but once on its south side one can head south-east into Coire Seasgach, following the stream to the little lochan which is its source on the north ridge of Bidein a' Choire Sheasgaich. There the previously described route is joined above the steep lower part of the ridge.

Sgurr na Feartag (862 m)

One final hill in this group may be mentioned as it gives a very pleasant short day's hill-walking from Achnashellach or Craig, namely Sgurr na Feartag. This is the long hill on the south side of Glen Carron which has some rather fine looking corries above the Achnashellach Forest. As the Ordnance Survey map indicates, there is a path right along the top of this hill from Glen Uig to Coire Leiridh, and this gives a very pleasant walk with, on a clear day, superb views of the mountains round Coire Lair on the opposite side of Glen Carron and the Torridonian giants beyond. The corries on the north side of this hill, Coire nan Each, Coire na h-Eilde and Coire Leiridh, all have quite steep headwalls, rocky in places, but there does not seem to be any possibility of worthwile climbing in summer. In winter it is possible that the bigger of the two gullies at the head of Coire Leiridh might give a fair climb in the right conditions. The path up the corrie goes very close to the foot of this gully.

Sgurr Mhuilinn (879 m)

Far to the north-east of the area just described stands Sgurr a' Mhuilinn. This rather isolated mountain consists of several pointed peaks which are conspicuous from several viewpoints. For example, from the south side of the Moray Firth, looking north-west, Sgurr a' Mhuilinn is just about the most prominent mountain on the horizon. It consists of a ridge running roughly from south-east to north-west with the highest point near its middle. To its north-west are Sgurr a' Ghlas Leathaid (844 m) and (unnamed on the Ordnance Survey map) Sgurr a' Choire Rainich, of almost equal height. South of the highest point, and separated from it by the Coire a' Mhuilinn, is Meallan nan Uan (840 m) flanked by the lesser points of Creag Ghlas and Creag Ruadh. The south and east sides of the mountain drop steeply into Strathconon and its offshoot Gleann Meinich, but the north and west slopes are featureless and degenerate into totally uninteresting moorland above Strath Bran.

The best starting point for the ascent of Sgurr a' Mhuilinn is at Strathanmore, a short distance up the strath from Milltown. Climb steeply up the grassy hillside on the south of the Allt an t-Srathain Mhoir until the flat corrie is reached, then cross the gently rising elevated peat bog north-westwards to the foot of the steep ridge leading to Sgurr a' Mhuilinn, which is climbed direct to the top. One can now make either a short or a long circuit of the other peaks. The short traverse involves descending south-west round the head of Coire a' Mhuilinn to climb Meallan nan Uan and continue along the pleasant narrow ridge to Creag Ruadh from where a descent north-eastwards brings one back to Strathanmore. The longer traverse involves a fairly long walk along the broad ridge to the two north-western outliers, and back again.

Creag Ghlas is the one peak that is of particular interest to rock-climbers as it has a huge craggy south-west face above Gleann Meinich, which is reached by a 4 km walk up this glen from Strathconon. From the climbing point of view the crag does not quite live up to the expectations generated by its fine appearance. There are two buttresses; the East Buttress is about 250 m high, but is ill-defined and grassy; the West Buttress is about 150 m high and is steep, compact and slabby, the rock being immaculately sound, but lacking holds and almost totally devoid of belays.

On the East Buttress, which is roughly triangular in shape, the left edge has been climbed by various routes between Difficult and Very Severe standard, depending upon whether or not the difficulties were climbed or avoided. The length is 250 m, and a detailed description is unnecessary on account of the amount of variation that is possible. On the right side of the East Buttress there is a longer climb by M. Birch and J. Mackenzie, *Boulder and Bolder* (330 m, Very Severe). The climb starts at a cairn below a short wall at the base of the buttress where terraces cross above smaller crags on the right. Climb the wall and rib above to take an optional crack on the left, or go right and climb pleasant rocks leading to a ledge and cairn below a steep slab. Climb the central crack (VS), then go right to pale rocks and up to easier ground. The climb continues towards a finely shaped arête, following a natural line up this arête and corners and cracks above it. (S.M.C.J., Vol. XXIX, No. 159, p. 63; Vol. XXIX, No. 161, p. 319; Vol. XXXI, No. 170, p. 408).

On the West Buttress the original route done by D. Bathgate and R. N. Campbell in 1967 is *The Lizard* (150 m, Very Severe). A prominent rib divides the buttress into smooth slabs on the left and steep walls and grassy corners on the right. The route follows this rib, keeping to the crest for two pitches as far as a broad rock terrace, and then climbing an enormous slab in two more 30 m pitches up its right edge to a glacis from which a final steep wall leads to the top. This route can be recommended as the best on the whole crag. Two more recent routes on the West Buttress are *Sweet Charity* by J. Mackenzie and D. Butterfield (115 m, Hard Very Severe) which is to the right of the central rib of The Lizard, and *Spare Rib* by R. McHardy and J. Mackenzie (70 m, Very Severe) which is on the right edge of the buttress. (S.M.C.J., Vol. XXIX, No. 159, p. 61; Vol. XXXII, No. 171, p. 59; Vol. XXXII, No. 172, p. 155).

Walks and Paths

The main east to west route through the area covered by this chapter is that from Glen Strathfarrar to Glen Carron. From Monar Lodge at the east end of Loch Monar a good path leads along the north shore of the loch to a point opposite Pait Lodge, 5 km from the west end of the loch. These 5 km are trackless, but the going is fairly easy on grass to the head of the loch where there is a choice of routes. The shortest leads to Craig in Glen Carron over the Bealach Bhearnais (there is a path for a short distance beyond the head of the loch). From the bealach the stalker's path down to Glen Uig and finally the good track in this glen are followed to Craig (26 km). An alternative from the Bealach Bhearnais is to go down the Abhainn Bhearnais to the bothy and from there either take the path to Achnashellach (30 km), or to Strathcarron (32 km).

The Bealach an Sgoltaidh offers a shorter but rather rougher route between the head of Loch Monar and Bearnais bothy.

The Strathconon to Glen Carron walk calls for no detailed description, following as it does the rather monotonous length of Gleann Fhiodhaig from Scardroy to Glenuaig Lodge where the track to Craig is joined (23 km).

Obviously various permutations of these routes can be made; for example between Loch Monar and Glenuaig Lodge by Srath Mhuilich, and between Loch Monar and Gleann Fhiodhaig by Coire Fionnarach.

Rock Climbing

There are a number of low-level crags near the foot of Strathconon, and a large crag at Raven's Rock to the north-west of Strathpeffer. These crags provide the most accessible rock-climbing in the area covered by this guide book, probably the most accessible in the north of Scotland. All have been explored by J. Mackenzie and his companions, and the following descriptions are taken from Mackenzie's contribution to the Scottish Mountaineering Club Journal (Vol. XXXII, No. 172) and further information communicated to the author.

The first is a small crag of sound schist on the south side of Loch Meig in Strathconon, 1 km west of the dam at Map Ref. 366557, and close to the road. Three routes have been recorded by D. McCallum and J. Mackenzie.

Meig Corner 30 m   Mild Very Severe
The obvious deep corner with a tree at its base. Gain the tree and continue up the fine corner to belays below the top bulge. Surmount the bulge (crux) to easy ground. Recommended.

The Balence 30 m   Very Severe
Climb the awkward rust coloured corner to the right of Meig Corner to a tree belay. Climb the arête on the right to gain a huge block. Climb the crux slab above. A good route.

Shy Bride's Crack 16 m   Extremely Severe E2
To the right of The Balence is a slab topped by a leaning wall split by a crack. Climb the slab easily, then the off-width crack with difficulty. Crux at top.

Glenmarksie Crag (From S.M.C.J., Vol. XXXII, No. 172)

On the opposite side of Strathconon, near the dam at the foot of Loch Luichart, is the Glenmarksie Crag at Map Ref. 384582. The crag is approached by a short walk up the hillside from the dam, to which one can drive. The crag is visible from the dam; it takes the form of a central slab steepening to a wall, bounded on the right by a slab and headwall. Two small crags lie above and to the right.

On the left of the main face the crag has a steep gully and a small buttress on the left rises above a rowan tree. Left of the tree, the rocks are little more than 10–15 m but of immaculate quality, giving numerous climbs. *Small Wall*, above the rowan tree has been climbed by a number of lines.

The first climbs described lie on the *Main Face*.

Dog Mantle   30 m   Severe

The route starts from half way up the gully separating *Small Wall* from the *Main Face*.

Traverse right to belays above in wide crack. Go straight up the steep wall to a corner left of large overhang and onto top.

Dog-Leg   43 m   Very Difficult

The slabs right of the gully are bordered by a rust coloured corner with a rose bush.

Up past bush and flake and mossy ledges to gain belays in wide crack as for *Dog Mantle*. Climb wall right of crack (as for *Dog Mantle*) then step left by horizontal break to gain niche. A large head of rock (*Dog Head*) has a vee corner on its right. Climb this to finish. A good top pitch.

The Juggler   33 m   Hard Very Severe

Start right of *Dog Leg* where a tongue of rock comes low down and is bounded on the right by a corner.

Climb right edge of slab to step left beneath overlaps then up to large block belays on left. Step right then up steep wall to mantleshelf, go left to block belays. Climb corner above past mantleshelf, step right to heather, then easily left to wide crack belays as for *Dog Mantle*. Climb up to inset right corner below big roof. Step around edge to gain sloping shelf (crux). Climb steep slab above to finish.

An excellent top pitch and recommended despite vegetation lower down.

Walking past a vegetated slab, there is a wedge of rock with a tree crowned ledge above.

Wild Mint   52 m   Mild Very Severe
Climb right-hand corner of block past roof to gain tree. From the tree step left and gain niche and climb slab rightwards to a break to reach broken ledges on left. Gain slab groove on left to ledges, from there go left to steep corner and up this to finish by large loose slab resting on top.

Walk on By   36 m   Very Severe
Climb the pod on the left side of wedge to the tree and belay. Traverse right across ledges to step up at end. Climb fine bald slab directly (crux) to reach niche of *Wild Mint*. Finish up this to escape right at ledge. Recommended.

Dynamite   36 m   Extremely Severe (E1)
To the right of the wedge is a black recess topped by overhangs.
   Up slab corner on right to surmount overlap. Step left and gain sloping ledges on left (crux). Finish by climbing *Walk on By's* fine slab directly above. Recommended.

Proteus   42 m   Hard Very Severe
Climb the groove right of *Dynamite*.
   Gain the ramp and step right under roof. Surmount and climb left rib to step right to gain niche (crux). Up thin groove above to roof and climb over this. Step up right to gain a shelf, then go up left past thin flake foothold to a small ledge. Step up right below upper slab. Climb upper slab directly.
   Recommended, a very concentrated first pitch which is well protected.

Greased Lightning   45 m   Hard Very Severe
The central wall is split by a prominent slanting groove. Start below this in a hollow where a heather bush grows below a zig-zag crack.
   Surmount flake and climb cracks above to glacis and belay in corner. At back of glacis is a corner crack, up this to step left (crux) to gain open chimney. Up this past constriction to top and exit left to tree. Two excellent pitches which are well protected. Highly recommended.

Direct Start   Hard Very Severe
Climb the pinnacle left of the normal start to gain bald slab and glacis.

Six Trees   31 m   Mild Very Severe
Right of *Greased Lightning* is a slab and corner. Up slab and crux corner, to gain large slab and belays. Traverse more easily right below headwall to finish.

Hiroshima Grooves   31 m   Extremely Severe (E1)
Start right of *Six Trees*, below the big slab and climb up slab to below nick in headwall near the corner of *Six Trees*. Surmount overhanging wall above to break and finish up this groove.

   To the right and above *Main Face* there is a crag, *Middle Crag*, which offers short slabby climbs and further to the right still is to be found *Top Crag*. It has an extensive overhanging face bordered on the right by a pinnacle which has also been climbed.

Moy Rock

   Moy Rock is the prominent cliff of Old Red Sandstone which faces south above the ruins of Brahan Castle at Map Ref. 512554. The cliff is vertical and rather featureless, and the obvious breaks tend to be vegetatious. The rock should be treated with great care, as the pebbles upon which one has to rely may not be well embedded in the conglomerate rock, although they may seem to be firm enough. This feature, coupled with the general lack of protection, gives the climbs a serious character. The following routes are described from left to right. In the centre of the face, well seen from the road, is a bird limed wall. It is separated from the main cliff by two bounding fault lines, the left one bordering a slab. Left again is a steep wall with a deep slabby ramp forming an open corner on its left.

Harderthanitlookscrack   40 m   Severe
The long ramp provides slab and corner climbing, vegetated at the top.

Slanting Crack   40 m   Difficult (Hard)
This route takes the left bounding fault of *Bird Lime Buttress*, and is a deep chimney-crack. Follow the deep crack left of the slab over chockstones to a bay. Straddle the chimney to a ledge. Climb the short wall above on the left to the top. Interesting, but not serious.

Boggle   48 m   Mild Very Severe
To the right of the last climb is a slab. Start by a curving groove and crack at its base to gain the open slab right of *Slanting Crack*. Climb the slab centrally to belays on the left below the top wall. Climb the steep

plinth right of centre in an exposed position to reach an easy arête. Descend at the far end to a ledge and finish up *Slanting Crack*.

Speliological Nightmare   30 m   Difficult (Hard)
To the right of *Bird Lime Buttress* is a leftward slanting chimney, and to its right is a broader tree-filled one. Start in the left chimney, up a groove and through a tunnel to a cave and belays. Struggle through the hole above to reach a saddle. Finish up a wide crack to belays below the final wall of *Slanting Crack* and climb that.

Magnificrack   45 m   Extremely Severe E2
To the right of the tree-filled chimney is a curving flake crack leading up to a vertical wall. Climb the bulging flake and gain the apex (running belay). Follow a small ragged crack up the wall above to its end. Climb the exposed crux wall to a horizontal break below the overhang. Take this on the left and climb a slab above to a small tree. Belay on a larger tree on the left. Continue up the short wall above the small tree to the top. A magnificent and serious climb.

Perigrination   40 m   Very Severe
Climb a bulge well to the right of *Magnificrack* to reach a vegetated bay. Exit on the wall right of the crack.

Ravens Rock (From S.M.C.J., Vol. XXXII, No. 172)

For reasons of conservation, this impressive schist crag must not be climbed on from May to July. It lies 1½ km west of Auchterneed Station on the Dingwall to Kyle line and 8 km from Dingwall. Access can be gained either by walking along the track or else leaving cars at Auchterneed Hamlet and walking west along a private road to join the line ½ km short of the crag.

The crag is extensive and stretches for 600 m. Facing north, there is a great deal of vegetation and all the lines needed cleaning prior to ascent, as will future routes. The cliff is in two parts. The top overhanging section of blackish rock has a table of grass which slopes down below it to a shorter overhanging wall. The top crag stretches westward and attains a height in excess of 100 m where it breaks into a series of grass ledges. Beyond lie roofs and cracks bordering a steep buttress which is in turn bounded by corner. A black wall beyond is cut by a ramp and further steep walls lead to a vertical roof-topped corner. A white wall and black wall separated by a tree crowned ledge diminish in height westwards where the crag outcrops through dense vegetation.

The escape route off the climbs lies behind the white wall and takes the form of a shallow gully, easy but vegetated.

The climbing is on very steep but generally sound rock which has had areas of loose blocks. Unclimbed lines may be superficially unsound. Nuts are well suited to the rocks and pegs are rarely needed.

Starting from the left end of the crag, which has hardly been touched, the number of routes multiply towards the cleaner right-end.

To make the first climb gain the grass table from the right to reach a minor jutting buttress beneath the great top wall. This small buttress has a central chimney.

Bone Idle   14 m   Hard Very Severe
Climb the thin crack right of the chimney to gain ledge on right; traverse left to finish up chimney.

A long section of unclimbed crag stretches to the great central buttress. The next line takes its left corner.

Scorpion   51 m   Mild Very Severe
Follow the corner to climb either slab or crack to gain fine cave formed by blocks. Belay. Step onto yardarm and climb overhung groove (crux) to mossy slabs and tree belays. Needs much more cleaning.

Tombstone Buttress   70 m   Extremely Severe (E1)
This fine climb takes the centre of the buttress. Start in the gloomy pit at the bottom right.

Climb black crack and roof above to slab. Go left across slab to chockstone and so to tree crowned ledge. A wall leads to a thin grass terrace. Go left to *Tombstone* and belay. Climb steep crack above to reach large block. Use the diagonal crack to traverse right and finally hand traverse to corner and spike. Up corner to belays by ledge. From ledge step left to crack splitting blocks and belay in *Scorpion* cave. Finish up *Scorpion*'s last pitch. Recommended.

Obituary   42 m   Extremely Severe (E1)
Start in the recessed corner of *Tombstone Buttress* and climb cracks on left to large roof. Traverse left to gain front of buttress and continue to thin crack. Up this (crux) to follow holds leading to a cracked bulge on the right of the buttress. Climb the exposed crack and bulge to belay

below third pitch of *Tombstone Buttress*; finish up this. Recommended, an excellent line.

Going right past the black corner and wall lies a long slab ramp.

The Sting   102 m   Hard Very Severe
Up slab to gain niche; surmount crux bulge on spikes to gain ramp. Follow ramp, taking the easiest line to small trees and belays. Climb easier cleaned slab to below overhung niche with tree above (arrow). Climb bulge and corner behind tree on vegetated rock, step right then up wall of cracked blocks to tree belays. Climb the steep awkward crack to a large birch tree to finish in the descent gully. A most enjoyable route which needs cleaning on the third pitch. Recommended.

Roots   66 m   Severe
To the right of *Sting* is a broken parallel groove. Climb it and traverse onto a good ledge and belays. Step up right onto a prominent spiky block (crux) and traverse a good slab rightwards. Near its end climb a cleaned wall to belay on *Sting* below its third pitch. Escape right along a vegetated ramp to gain the descent gully. A bit artificial but some pleasant climbing.

Shortly   15 m   Hard Very Severe
Right of *Roots* is an overhanging wall. Start below trees and gain right slanting line, surmounting crux bulge beyond treelet to go right to finish. Needs more cleaning.

Raspberry Traverse   45 m   Severe
Right of *Roots*, past the overhanging wall is an obvious corner. Climb it then go left and up short wall (crux) to belay below trees. Traverse right around corner and continue to small gnarled tree in an exposed position, to go up and left past niche to tree belays and scrambling above.

Jacobite Wall   48 m   Extremely Severe (E1)
Right of *Raspberry Traverse* is a steep wall bordered on the right by a grass mound which hides a fine cave.

Start left of cave and up steep wall past curious flake, step left to corner and up to ledge (crux) and flake. Step up right to long ledge and traverse right to break. Go up left to gain crack and up to small tired

159

tree and belays in crack behind. Climb easier cracked corner to finish as for *Raspberry Traverse*. Recommended.

Kingfisher   51 m   Hard Very Severe
Start at the raised grass mound and up short wall to follow crack to treelet, go back up left and mantleshelf onto unhelpful slab (crux). Step up right and then directly up wall, which eases after the initial moves, to belays well left of the big roof along ledge. Follow a diagonal line up the overhanging head wall in a good position, starting at the left by blocks to reach jutting ledge. Step left to finish up short wall to trees above.
An excellent and popular line. Recommended.

The Croak   51 m   Hard Very Severe
Climb the steep corner right of *Kingfisher* which gives some awkward moves to reach a sloping grass ledge, belays at back. Climb cracked slab to swing round edge and tree belay above. Climb wall above tree, finding the easiest line, to top.
A good first pitch, the last pitch needs cleaning and can be avoided by traversing off right. Recommended.

Fancy Tickler   30 m   Very Severe
To the right of the *Croak* is a steep wall split by three cracks. Climb the short left one to grass ledge and tree belay. Climb the thin crack right of the arête, crux, to trend left to tree and belays as for *Croak*.
Well protected and sustained.

Close to the Edge   48 m   Hard Very Severe
Climb the central crack in the wall, crux, tree belay above. Gain a ledge and go up and right to niche, exit from this step right and up a crack to ledge and tree belay as for *Croak*. Finish up the mossy wall as for *Croak*, or escape right along ledge.
Pleasant, well protected climbing.

Ravens Horror   12 m   Hard Very Severe
Climb the third crack which lies centrally in the wall to a jutting hold. Traverse out right along to edge and up to tree belay. Poor protection.

Ravens Squawk   90 m   Mild Very Severe
The length excludes easy ground.

160

Climb the slab and corner which lie right of *Ravens Horror* to the ledge and tree belay. Gain the ledge and climb the wall just right of the niche of *Close to the Edge*, to gain old peg belays in alcove. Climb up to the crack in the roof above and exit left of sapling. Climb mossy wall direct to gain the descent gully. Scramble across gully to the back tier of cliffs. Climb on set smooth slab and step across a bigger slab to tree. Easily up descent gully until a shallow groove on right is climbed to heather ledge. Traverse along this to vee crack and exit.

An artificial ramble with some enjoyable moments. Loose rock on pitch 3 needs cleaning. The first route on the crag.

Archenemy
To the right of *Ravens Squawk* is a cleaned slab with a crack splitting a steep wall above. Climb the crack to small tree and niche. Move right to ledge (crux), then along corner and up this to finish. Very deceptive and recommended as a painless introduction to the crag.

The Corner   15 m   Very Difficult
Up slab, then up right corner.

Rejector   18 m   Mild Very Severe
An amusing problem right of *The Corner*, where a slabby V-groove lies right of a short steep wall. Up wall to enter groove, awkward, then easily to top. Traditionally climbed in unsuitable footwear.

The wall to the right has a short Very Difficult groove. Walk round the edge to an open chimney.

The Chimney   10 m   Severe
Climb the chimney, exit left, swing back right to finish up a corner.

Cavalcade Wall   18 m   Severe
Climb the descent gully (which lies beyond *The Chimney*) to near a fallen tree, below which is a white wall with a central niche. Climb up past niche to level with tree then exit left.

There are many short problems to the right on the small outcrops.

Ravens Rock Quarry

This lies a $\frac{1}{2}$ km beyond Ravens Rock, heading west. It is very loose and gives some climbing on the smooth slab on the right.

Pad Slab   30 m   Severe

Towards the right of the slab to a tree crowned ledge. Gain this and up slab and groove above the tree to top, trending left

The slab has been climbed direct and has several lines. The corners to the left are about Very Difficult in standard.

The centre of the quarry provides a 33 m Grade IV ice climb *Centre Fall* when frozen.

Red Rock

A small but imposing schist crag $\frac{3}{4}$ km east of Ravens. It is best approached by a break in the forestry plantations near the end of the road. Possibilities are limited due to its triangular aspect but has one central climb. Like Ravens there is no climbing from May–July.

Red Wall Grooves   33 m   Very Severe

The centre of the face has a prominent curving groove line. Start from the ledge below where a mass of ivy festoons the left side of the roofs above.

Climb up to roof and traverse right to a break then step left to a ledge and belays on the right. At the left end of ledge go up to holds and up the crux wall trending slightly right past jug to enter niche. Continue up the curving groove to the top.

An exciting climb, appearing larger than it is. Recommended.

Place names and their meanings

The following list contains a selection of the more important place names mentioned in the book, the spellings being those given in the latest edition of the Ordnance Survey maps. The meanings of the names are those given in the previous edition of the Western Highlands District Guide, from which the list has been abstracted in full.

In general, 'Bh' or 'Mh' equals 'V' while 'Fh' is silent as is 'dh' and 'th', 'S' after an t' is silent.

A' Chràlaig: (*should be* A' Chràileag), the circular place (*Chrawley*).
A' Ghlas-bheinn: the green mountain.
Allt a' Ghlomaich: the stream of the gloomy hollow or chasm.
Am Bàthaich: the byre (bay).
An Diollaid: the saddle.
An Eag: the notch.
An Leth-Chreag: the half rock.
An Riabhachan: the brindled hill.
An t-Slat-bheinn: the wand mountain.
An Socach: the snout.
An Stac: the stack.
Aonach air Chrith: the shaking height.
Aonach Meadhoin: the middle height (*vane*).
Aonach Sgoilte: the split height (*sgoiltsh*).

Bealach Bhearnais: the pass of the gap.
Bealach Coire Sgoir-adail: (*should be* Sgoradail), the pass of the corrie of the
    sharp peak.
Bealach Duibh Leac: the pass of the black flagstones.
Bealach an Fhìona: the pass of the wine.
Bealach an t-Sealgaire: the pass of the hunter.
Bealach an Sgàirne: the pass of rumbling.
Bealach an Sgoltaidh: the pass of the splitting.
Ben Aden: the mountain of the face.

Beinn a' Bha' ach Ard: the mountain of the high byre (?).
Beinn Fhada: (*should be* A' Beinn Fhada), the long mountain (*atta*).
Beinn Fhionnlaidh: Findlay's mountain.
Beinn Gharbh: the rough mountain.
Ben Hiant: (*i.e.* Beinn Shianta), the holy mountain.
Beinn Mheadhoin: the middle mountain.
Beinn na Muice: the mountain of the pig.
Beinn Odhar Bheag: the little dun mountain (*ower veg*).
Beinn Odhar Mhòr: the big dun mountain.
Ben Resipol: *doubtful* (pol = O.N., ból, bólstaðr, a homestead).
Beinn na Seilg: (*should be* Beinn na Seilge), the mountain of hunting.
Ben Sgritheall: *doubtful* (*screel*).
Ben Tee: the mountain of the fairy hillock.
Beinn Tharsuinn: (*should be* Beinn Tarsuinn), the cross mountain.
Beinn an Tuim: the mountain of the hillock.
Bidein a' Choire Sheasgaich: the little peak of the reedy corrie.
Bidean an Eòin Deirg: the little peak of the red bird.
Bràigh a' Choire Bhig: the top of the little corrie.

Càrn an Daimh Bhàin: the cairn of the white stag.
Càrn Eige: the cairn of the notch.
Càrn nam Fiaclan: the cairn of the teeth.
Càrn Ghluasaid: the cairn of moving (*ghlushat*).
Càrn nan Gobhar: the cairn of the goats (*gower*).
Ceum na h-Aon-choise: the step for one foot.
Ciste Dhubh: the black chest (*kistehoo*).
Coire nan Dearcag: the corrie of the berries (*yercag*).
Coire Dhorrcail: (Coire Thorcuill?), Torquil's corrie (*horcal*).
Coire Domhain: the deep corrie (*dovun*).
Coire an Iubhair: the corrie of the yew tree (*yewver*).
Creach Bheinn: *probably* the denuded peak (creachan = the bare windswept top of hill).
Creag a' Chaoruinn: the rock of the rowan tree.
Creag a' Choir' Aird: the rock of the high corrie.
Creag nan Clachan Geala: the rock of the white stones.
Creag nan Damh: the rock of the stag.
Creag Dhubh: the black rock.
Creag na h-Eige: the rock of the notch.
Creag Ghlas: the grey rock.
Creag Ghorm a' Bhealaich: the blue rock of the pass.
Creag a' Mhàim: the breast rock.
Creag Ruadh: the red rock.
Creag Toll a' Choin: the rock of the dog's den.
Culvain—*see* Gulvain.

Druim Chòsaidh: the ridge with nooks or crevices (*hosey*).
Druim Fiaclach: the toothed ridge.
Druim Shionnach: the ridge of the foxes.

Faochag: the whelk.
Fàradh Nighean Fhearchair: the ladder of Farquhar's daughter (*nine*).
Fuar-thol Mòr: the big cold hole.

Gairich: the peak of yelling.
Garbh Bheinn: the rough mountain.
Garbh-chàrn: the rough cairn.
Garbh Chìoch Bheag: the little rough pap.
Garbh Chìoch Mhòr: the big rough pap.
Garbh Choire Beag: the little rough corrie.
Garbh Choire Mòr: the big rough corrie.
Gleouraich: uproar.
Gulvain or Gaor Bheinn: thrill mountain (?).

Ladhar Bheinn: the forked mountain (*La'arven*).
Loch Beoraid: the beaver loch (?).
Lochan nam Breac: the little loch of the trout.
Luinne Bheinn: *doubtful.*
Lurg Mhòr: the big shank.

Màm na Cloich' Airde: (*should be* Mam na Clochairde), the rounded hill of the
   stony height.
Mam Sodhail: (*should be* Mam Sabhal), the rounded hill of barns (*Sowl*).
Maol Chinn-dearg: (*should be* Maol Cheann-dearg), the bald red-headed hill.
Maoile Lunndaidh: the hill of the boggy place.
Maol Odhar: the dun bald hill (*ower*).
Meall a' Bhealaich: the lump of the pass.
Meall Buidhe: the yellow lump (*booy*).
Meallan Buidhe: the little yellow lump.
Meall a' Chreagain Duibh: the lump of the little black rock.
Meal Dearg Choire nam Muc: the lump of the red corrie of the swine.
Meall Mòr: the big lump.
Meall an Tàrmachain: the lump of the ptarmigan.
Meall na Teanga: the lump of the tongue (*changa*).
Meallan nan Uan: the little lump of the lambs.
Meall an Uillt Chaoil: the lump of the narrow burn.
Moruisg: *doubtful.*
Morvern: the sea gap.
Morvich: the sea plain.
Mullach Fraoch-choire: the top of the heather corrie.

Plaide Mhòr: the big flat.

Rois-bheinn: (*almost certainly* Froisbheinn), the mountain of the showers.
Rudha na Spréidhe: the point of the herd (*spray*).

Sàileag: the little heel.
Saoiter Mòr: the big soldier (?).

M

Sgùman Còinntich: the mossy stack (*sgooman*).
Sgùrr na h-Aide: the peak of the hat (*sgoor na h'Atch*).
Sgùrr Àiridh na Beinne: the peak of the shieling by the peak (*arry*).
Sgùrr na Bà Glaise: the peak of the grey cow.
Sgùrr Beag: the little peak.
Sgùrr a' Bhealaich Dheirg: the peak of the red gap.
Sgùrr na Càrnach: the peak of the stony place.
Sgùrr nan Ceannaichean: the peak of the merchants.
Sgùrr nan Ceathreamhnan: (*should be* Ceathramhnan), the peak of the quarters (*Kerranan*).
Sgùrr a' Chaorachain: the peak of the white, boiling, tumbling torrent.
Sgùrr a' Chlaidheimh: the peak of the sword (*cleeve*).
Sgùrr Choinnich: the mossy peak.
Sgùrr na Ciche: the pap-shaped peak.
Sgùrr na Ciste Duibhe: the peak of the black chest (*kiste dooy*).
Sgùrr nan Clachan Geala: the peak of the white stones.
Sgùrr à Choire-bheithe: the peak of the birch corrie (*vey*).
Sgùrr Coire Chòinnichean: the peak of the mossy corrie.
Sgùrr nan Coireachan: the peak of the corries.
Sgùrr Coire na Feinne: the peak of the corrie of the warrior band.
Sgùrr a' Choire Ghairbh: the peak of the rough corrie.
Sgùrr a' Choire Ghlais: the peak of the green corrie.
Sgùrr a' Choire-rainich: the peak of the dripping, or bracken, corrie.
Sgùrr nan Conbhairean: the peak of the dog-men.
Sgùrr na Creige: the peak of the rock.
Sgùrr Dhomhnuill: Donald's peak.
Sgòrr na Diòllaid: the peak of the saddle.
Sgùrr an Doire Leathain: the peak of the broad thicket.
Sgùrr a' Dubhdoire: the peak of the black copse.
Sgùrr na h-Eanchainne: the peak of the brains.
Sgùrr nan Eugallt: the peak of the death precipices (?).
Sgùrr na Fearstaig: (*should be* Sgùrr nam Feartag), the peak of the sea pinks.
Sgùrr an Fhuarail: the peak of the cold place (*ooral*).
Sgùrr an Fhuarain: *doubtful* (*oorain*).
Sgùrr Fhuaran: *doubtful*.
Sgùrr Fhuar-thuill: the peak of the cold hole.
Sgùrr na Forcan: the forked peak.
Sgùrr a' Gharg Gharaidh: the peak of the rough den.
Sgùrr Ghiubhsachain: the peak of the fir wood (*goosachan*).
Sgùrr a' Ghlas Leathaid: the peak of the grey hillside (*le'ad*).
Sgùrr na Làpaich: the peak of the bog.
Sgùrr Leac nan Each: the peak of the flat rock of the horses.
Sgùrr an Lochain: the peak of the little loch.
Sgùrr a' Mhaoraich: the peak of the shell-fish.
Sgòr Mhic Eacharna: MacEchern's peak.
Sgùrr a' Mhuilinn: the peak of the mill (*voolin*).
Sgùrr Mòr: the great peak.
Sgùrr na Mòraich: the peak of the sea plain.

Sgùrr na Muice: the peak of the pig.
Sgùrr Nid na h-Iolaire: the peak of the eagle's nest.
Sgùrr Rainich: (*should be* Ronnaich), the dripping peak.
Sgùrr na Ruaidhe: the peak of the red (hind or cow).
Sgùrr nan Saighead: the peak of the arrows (*sight, approx.*).
Sgùrr an t-Searraich: the peak of the foal.
Sgùrr Sgiath Airidh: (probably Sgitharigh), the peak of Skiði's shieling (*skee'ary*).
Sgùrr na Sgine: the peak of the knife (*sgeen*).
Sgùrr nan Spainteach: the peak of the Spaniards.
Sgùrr Thionail: the peak of the gathering.
Sgùrr Thuilm: the peak of the holm (*hoolm*).
Sgùrr an Utha: the peak of the udder.
Sìthean na Raplaich: the fairy hill of the screes.
Spidean Dhomhuill Bhric: speckled Donald's pinnacle.
Spidean Mialach: the pinnacle of wild animals, *e.g.* hares.
Sròn a' Choire Ghairbh: the nose of the rough corrie.
Sròn Gharbh: the rough nose.
Sròn a' Gharbh Choire Bhig: the nose of the little rough corrie.
Stob a' Chearcaill: the spike of the circle (*heercal*).
Stob Coire nan Cearc: the spike of the hens' corrie, *i.e.* grouse.
Stob a' Choire Odhair: the spike of the dun corrie (*ower*).
Streap: climbing.
Streap Comhlaidh: climbing (adjoining ?).
Stùc Bheag: the little peak.
Stùc Mòr: the big peak.

Tigh Mòr na Seilge: the big house of the hunting.
Toll Creagach: the rocky hole.
Tom a' Chòinich: (*should be* Tom Chóinnich), the mossy hillock.

Uisge Misgeach: the water of intoxication (*oosgy misgy*).

APPENDIX II

The wanderings of Prince Charles Edward Stuart after the Battle of Culloden

A. E. Robertson

The Battle of Culloden was fought on the 16th of April 1746. It began at one o'clock, and in half an hour the Jacobite forces were routed and the Prince was forced to flee to the Western Highlands to reach France and safety.

Crossing the River Nairn at the ford of Faillie, accompanied by a small band of half a dozen horsemen, he took the road up Strath Nairn by Tordarroch to Aberarder and then over into Strath Errick and on to Gorthlick, a house on the west side of Loch Mhor. Here old Simon Fraser, Lord Lovat, was awaiting news of the battle; the arrival of the Prince in full flight must have disconcerted that crafty old gentleman not a little. Riding on through the night by the then existing Wade road up Strath Errick, the Prince reached Fort Augustus and then on to Invergarry, where he arrived in the early hours of the 17th April.

Resting there till the afternoon, the Prince with three faithful followers set out again, and taking the old bridle track on the west side of Loch Lochy he made for the west end of Loch Arkaig by Clunes, the Dark Mile and Murlaggan, eventually finding shelter for the night at the home of Donald Cameron of Glen Pean. The evening of the next day saw the Prince on the move again. He was now on foot as the Braes of Morar were too rough for horses. It must have been heavy going then, as it is now, up Glen Pean by the boggy, squelching track over the bealach and down to Oban at the east end of Loch Morar.

On the night of the 20th he walked to Borrodale, on the north shore of Loch nan Uamh, via Glen Beasdale and he set sail on the 26th for

Benbecula in the Outer Hebrides. Then followed for the Prince many weeks of sore privations and hairbreadth escapes in Benbecula, Scalpay and Loch Boisdale. Eventually, near Ormaclett on the west coast of South Uist, he met Flora Macdonald, and had it not been for the clever resource of that brave lady he would undoubtedly have been captured, hemmed in as he then was by Government troops and the ever-vigilant Government navy. Securing a pass for herself and her maid, she dressed the Prince up in female attire as Betty Burke, and in this disguise she managed to smuggle him across the Minch in a boat, landing at Kilbride in Trotternish, Skye on the 29th of June. She then took him to Kingsburgh House and the next day, at Portree, he said farewell to his brave rescuer. After a day in the Island of Raasay with two or three followers and guides, he got back to near Portree and, after skirting past the head of Loch Sligachan, he eventually reached Elgol on the east shore of Loch Scavaig where he took a boat for the mainland.

On 5th July the Prince landed at Mallaigvaig and found shelter at Cross, a mile south of the bridge over the Morar River. Thence he went to a cave on the shore below Borrodale House. On 13th July he moved to Macleod's Cove, 'upon a high precipice in the woods of Borrodale', and on the 17th to MacEachine's Refuge, high up in a corrie about $1\frac{1}{2}$ km north of the west end of Loch Eilt, overlooking Loch Beoraid.

Endeavouring to escape through the line of camps and sentries that had by then been established from the head of Loch Eil to the head of Loch Hourn, the Prince's route was briefly as follows:—East by Sgurr a' Mhuidhe to Fraoch-bheinn, then north through Coire Odhar to Glen Pean, and still north to upper Glen Dessarry, Coire nan Gall and a 'fast place' at the west end of Loch Quoich, reached in the early hours of 20th July.

Leaving at eight o'clock that night, the Prince and his party, six in all, climbed to the top of Meall an Spardain and observed the enemy's camps close below them at the foot of Gleann Cosaidh. Creeping down to the foot of the glen, they skulked across above and within the line of the said camps. They then climbed up the hill immediately in front of them (Leac na Fearna), then down into Coire Beithe and, in the early morning of the 21st, they passed between two of the sentries in Corrie Hoo (probably just to the south of Loch Coire Shubh), thus breaking through the cordon that had hemmed them in Clanranald's country.

Reaching Coire Sgoireadail, they spent the day in 'a bit of hollow ground with long heather and branches of young birch trees', in full view of the soldiers encamped at the very head of Loch Hourn. Setting out that night, they stumbled up Coire Sgoireadail in pitch darkness, and over the Bealach Duibh Leac down to Glen Shiel, where they found shelter for the day behind a great boulder on the north side of the river about $1\frac{1}{2}$ km south-east of Achnangart. This boulder is well known to the local inhabitants, and it is pointed out as 'Prince Charlie's Stone'. Turning eastwards they made for Strath Glass by Glen Shiel and Strath Cluanie, spending a night near the summit of Sgurr nan Conbhairean 'wet to the skin and devoured by midges'.

On 24th July they fell in with the famous eight Glen Moriston men who had fought for the Prince at Culloden and had taken refuge in a cave in Coire Mheadhoin, at the head of Coire Dho in Ceannacroc. This cave is well worth a visit. It resembles the Shelter Stone in the Cairngorms, being formed of several large boulders massed together which have fallen from the rocks of Tigh Mor na Seilge.

In this cave the Prince stayed for a week, and on the first day of August, starting at night, he and his whole party crossed over to Athnamulloch at the west end of Loch Affirc, thence eastwards down Glen Affric to the Braes of Strathglass, finding shelter in a 'Sheally hut' in the depths of the Fasnakyle woods. They then moved on into Glen Cannich, and climbed to the crest of the ridge between Meallan Odhar and An Soutar, just north of Liatrie, in the hope of meeting a messenger who had been sent to Poolewe for tidings of the French ship there. This was the most northerly point that Prince Charles reached.

Receiving the intelligence that the ship at Poolewe had sailed, he resolved to make his way back to Locheil's country and on the 8th August, at night, they crossed the River Cannich at Muchrachd, then over by Fasnakyle, past Comar, Tomich, over the old drove road by Loch na Beinne Baine to the Braes of Glen Moriston. Then westwards up Glen Moriston, over to Loch Loyne by the River Loyne, and down to the Garry near Tomdoun. Fording the Garry with difficulty, they travelled across the hills to Achnasaul on Loch Arkaig, which they reached on 15th August. In this neighbourhood the Prince spent nearly a fortnight, hiding in sundry 'fast places'—one in Gleann Cia-aig, another in the Dark Mile and another in Torr a' Mhuilt.

On 28th August the Prince set forth for Badenoch to join Locheil and Cluny Macpherson, travelling by the headwaters of the Roy, over the ridge of Creag Meaghaidh (probably through the Window), down Coire Arder and so to Ardverikie, eventually finding shelter with Locheil and Cluny Macpherson in Cluny's 'Cage', which had been constructed out of wood and moss in the high steep ground overlooking Loch Ericht, in the corrie above Benalder Cottage. There he remained for a week.

On 13th September, at one o'clock in the morning, hearing of the arrival of the French ships at Borrodale, the Prince started back again for the west. Crossing by the Allt a' Chaoil-reidhe and Loch a' Bhealaich Leamhain, he reached Moy at the west end of Loch Laggan, then up the Moy Burn, over the western ridge of Creag Meaghaidh and down by the Uisge nam Fichead to the head of Glen Roy. On the night of the 15th he crossed the River Lochy, and so to Achnacarry; then along the south side of Loch Arkaig to Gleann Camgharaidh. Spending the night there, he travelled on up Glen Pean, reaching Loch nan Uamh on 19th September 1746; there the Prince with a large party of his followers embarked on board a French ship and sailed for France.

A list of addresses of Estates, Factors and other useful addresses

The following list of estate addresses is taken from the document *Access for Mountain Climbers* published jointly by the Scottish Landowners' Federation and the Mountaineering Council of Scotland in 1981. The following notes are from the preamble to this document:—

1. Disturb open country as little as possible; avoid noise, and use established paths or similar routes where possible.

2. Walkers should avoid upsetting estate work, e.g. shooting, lambing, etc. by checking with estate staff. Useful information will be obtained from these sources, and good relations will be maintained if the restricted periods are observed.

3. Permission should be sought before camping or lighting a fire. It is an offence to light a fire without the landowner's permission, and camping without permission is also an offence.

4. Visitors should not use estate premises without permission. Bothies which have been made available with landowners' permission by arrangement with the Mountain Bothies Association are noted in this guide book. Visitors are reminded that bothies are not intended for club meets.

5. Cars should not be taken on private roads or ground without permission. When parking, do not obstruct gates or tracks.

6. In Scotland the situation as regards access to the mountains is more favourable than elsewhere in the U.K. One cannot be prosecuted for walking in open country, but one may be sued for damage arising from trespass.

The following list of addresses is not exhaustive. It contains only those which were contributed to the *Access for Mountain Climbers* document.

Attadale Estate, Loch Carron
E. A. Macpherson, Attadale Estate, c/o Bingham, Hughes and Macpherson, 45 Church Street, Inverness.
Local Contact: Tom Watson, Attadale, Strathcarron. Tel: Lochcarron 308.

Glenshiel Estate
Burton Property Trustees, Dochfour Estate Office, Inverness.
Local Contact: I. Campbell, Shiel House. Tel.: Glenshiel 282.

Kinlochhourn Estate
H. C. Birkbeck, Kinloch Hourn, Invergarry, Inverness-shire.

Arnisdale Estate
R. N. Richmond-Watson, Arnisdale, Kyle of Lochalsh, Inverness-shire.
Local Contact: I. McKenzie. Tel.: Glenelg 229.

Eilanreach Estate (south of Glenelg, includes Beinn Sgritheall)
M. Willis, Oversley Castle Farm, Wixford, Alcester, Warwickshire.
Local Contact: W. J. Macleod, Eilanreach, Glenelg, Kyle of Lochalsh, Inverness-shire. Tel.: Glenelg 244 (after 5 p.m.).

Balmacara—Kintail Estate
National Trust for Scotland, 5 Charlotte Square, Edinburgh.
Information Centre at Morvich, Strath Croe.

Affric Estate
Forestry Commission
Local Contact: D. MacLennan, Keeper's Cottage, Cannich.
J. MacLennan, Under Stalker, Comar Hill, Cannich. Tel.: Cannich 288.

Glen Pean
Possfund Pension Trust, per Fountain Forestry Limited, Perth.
Contact: Fountain Forestry Limited. Tel.: Inverness 224948.

Glen Dessarry
Lord Pollington, per Fountain Forestry Limited, Perth.
Contact: Mr. Ashmole, Fountain Forestry Limited, Perth. Tel.: Perth 28151.

173

Locheil Estates
Donald Cameron Yr. of Locheil, per J. P. S. Hunter, West Highland Estates Office, Fort William, Inverness-shire. Tel.: Fort William 2433.

Arisaig—Morar Estate
Miss M. J. Becher, Arisaig Estate, per J. P. S. Hunter, West Highland Estates Office, Fort William, Inverness-shire. Tel.: Fort William 2433.
Local Contact: E. D. MacMillan, Borrodale. Tel.: Arisaig 229.

Glen Aladale Estate
Lt. Col. L. Gray-Cheape, Carse Gray, Forfar, Angus.
Local Contact: R. Crocket, Glenfinnan. Tel.: Kinlocheil 241.
   (The use of the private bothy at Glenaladale may be arranged privately).

Glenmoidart Estate
J. Lees-Millais, Glenmoidart House, Kinlochmoidart, Inverness-shire.
Local Contact: Proprietor or Stalker, Glenmoidart House. Tel.: Salen 254.

Conaglen Estate
J. M. Guthrie of Conaglen, Ardgour, Inverness-shire, per R. T. Sidgwick, West Highland Estates Office, Fort William, Inverness-shire.
Local Contact: W. Ferguson, Stronchreggan, Conaglen, Ardgour. Tel.: Corpach 227.

Ardgour Estate
Miss Maclean of Ardgour, Ardgour, Fort William.
Local Contact: R. MacLean of Ardgour, Ardvullin, Ardgour. Tel.: Ardgour 224.

Inversanda Estate
Miss MacLean of Ardgour, Ardgour, Fort William.
Local Contact: Capt. E. A. S. Bailey, Inversanda, Ardgour.

Nature Conservancy Council
Fraser Darling House, 9 Culduthel Road, Inverness. Tel.: 0463 39431.

INDEX